MAXnotes®

Harper Lee's

To Kill a Mockingbird

Text by
Anita P. Davis
(Ed.D., Duke University)
Department of Education
Converse College
Spartanburg, South Carolina

Illustrations by
Michael A. Kupka

Research & Education Association
Visit our website at
www.rea.com

Research & Education Association
61 Ethel Road West
Piscataway, New Jersey 08854
E-mail: info@rea.com

MAXnotes® for
TO KILL A MOCKINGBIRD

Published 2017

Printed in the United States of America

Library of Congress Control Number 2003108319

ISBN-13: 978-0-87891-946-8
ISBN-10: 0-87891-946-5

What **MAXnotes**® *Will Do for You*

This book is intended to help you absorb the essential contents and features of Harper Lee's *To Kill a Mockingbird* and to help you gain a thorough understanding of the work. Our book has been designed to do this more quickly and effectively than any other study guide.

For best results, this **MAXnotes** book should be used as a companion to the actual work, not instead of it. The interaction between the two will greatly benefit you.

To help you in your studies, this book presents the most up-to-date interpretations of every chapter of the actual work, followed by questions and fully explained answers that will enable you to analyze the material critically. The questions also will help you to test your understanding of the work and will prepare you for discussions and exams.

Meaningful illustrations are included to further enhance your understanding and enjoyment of the literary work. The illustrations are designed to place you into the mood and spirit of the work's settings.

This **MAXnotes** book analyzes and summarizes each chapter as you go along, with discussions of the characters and explanations of the plot. A biography of the author and examination of the work's historical context will help you put this literary piece into the proper framework of what is taking place.

The use of this study guide will save you the hours of preparation time that would ordinarily be required to arrive at a complete grasp of this work of literature. You will be well prepared for classroom discussions, homework, and exams. The guidelines that are included for writing papers and reports on various topics will prepare you for any added work that may be assigned.

The **MAXnotes** will take your grades "to the max."

Larry B. Kling
Chief Editor

Contents

**Each chapter includes List of Characters,
Summary, Analysis, Study Questions and
Answers, and Suggested Essay Topics.**

A Glance at Some of the Characters

Scout Finch

Atticus Finch

Calpurnia

Boo Radley

Caroline Fisher

"Dill" Charles Harris

Jem Finch

Reverend Sykes

SECTION ONE

Introduction

The Life and Work of Harper Lee

Nelle Harper Lee was born on April 28, 1926 in Monroeville, Alabama, the daughter of Amas Coleman Lee (an attorney) and Frances Fincher Lee. Harper had one brother, Edwin.

As children, Harper and Edwin became good friends with Truman Capote, who would later become well-known for his book *In Cold Blood* and for his short stories and novels, including *Breakfast at Tiffany's*. Capote spent about six years with cousins in Monroeville after his parents' divorce. Capote was berated by his mother because he had effeminate mannerisms; the former Miss Alabama sent him off to be raised by various aunts, cousins, and his grandmother. It is quite possible that Capote was the model for the character Dill in Harper Lee's *To Kill a Mockingbird*.

Harper attended public schools in Monroeville and attended Huntington College in Montgomery from 1944–45. She spent the next four years at the University of Alabama where she studied law. Harper also spent one year at Oxford University.

Her education completed, Harper moved to New York, where she worked as a reservations clerk for Eastern Airlines and for British Overseas Airways in the 1950s. She gave up her job to devote her time to writing.

Harper wrote *To Kill a Mockingbird* (1960) very slowly. She usually began writing at noon and worked until evening; her goal was to complete only one or two pages per day. The book won her the

Pulitzer Prize (1961), the Alabama Library Association Award (1961), and the annual *Bestsellers'* paperback award (1962).

Horton Foote adapted the book into a movie. *The Motion Picture Guide*, Volume T-V, 1927-1983, states that the screenplay

> ...so wonderfully followed the spirit of Lee's novel that it prompted the author to remark, "I can only say that I am a happy author. They have made my story into a beautiful and moving motion picture. I am very proud and grateful.

The Academy of Motion Pictures presented Foote with the academy award for Best Adapted Screenplay. Gregory Peck starred as Atticus; he took the Academy Award for Best Actor.

To Kill a Mockingbird was the first—and last—book by Harper Lee.

Historical Background

To Kill a Mockingbird is set in Maycomb, a small Southern town in Alabama in the 1930s. The reader is not told the date until more than halfway through the book, but the references to the NRA, Hitler, and the quote "we have nothing to fear but fear itself" set the time in the reader's mind. The racially divided town and the strict class system help the reader to visualize life in the South during this time period.

Master List of Characters

Atticus Finch—*A Southern lawyer and the father of Scout and Jem.*

Scout Finch (also known as Jean Louise)—*Atticus' daughter. She is six years old when the story begins.*

Jem Finch (also known as Jeremy Atticus)—*Atticus' son, who is ready for fifth grade when the story begins.*

Charles Baker Harris (Dill)—*A six-year-old who visits his Aunt Rachel Haverford in Maycomb.*

Calpurnia and Zeebo—*The cook for the Finch family and her son, who also drives a garbage truck.*

Aunt Alexandra Hancock—*Atticus' sister, who is married to Jimmy*

Hancock. *She has one son named Henry and a seven-year-old grandson named Francis.*

Mr. and Mrs. Radley—*The parents of Arthur and Nathan Radley.*

Arthur Radley (a.k.a. "Boo Radley")—*A recluse in the neighborhood and the younger brother of Nathan Radley.*

Mr. Walter Cunningham and **Walter Cunningham**—*A proud but poor father and son. The son is Scout's classmate.*

Cecil Jacobs—*Scout's classmate.*

Mr. Robert Ewell—*The irresponsible father of Burns and Mayella. He spends his welfare checks on alcohol.*

Burns Ewell—*Robert Ewell's son who attends Scout's class for one day.*

Mayella Ewell—*Robert Ewell's daughter; she accuses Tom Robinson of raping her.*

Little Chuck Little—*A well-mannered classmate of Scout.*

Miss Carolina Fisher and **Miss Gates**—*Scout's first and third-grade teachers.*

Miss Maudie Atkinson—*A friend of Jem and Scout who lives up the street.*

Mrs. Henry Lafayette Dubose—*An elderly woman on Jem and Scout's street. They call her the "meanest old woman in the world."*

Miss Stephanie Crawford and **Mr. Avery**—*Two neighborhood gossips.*

Dr. Reynolds—*The family doctor.*

Eula May—*The telephone operator.*

Tom Robinson and **Helen Robinson**—*Husband and wife; Tom is accused of rape.*

Jack Finch—*Atticus's brother, who is a doctor.*

Heck Tate—*The sheriff.*

Lula—*An argumentative member of Calpurnia's church.*

Reverend Sykes—*Preacher of the First Purchase A.M.E. Zion Church.*

Mr. B. B. Underwood—*Editor of* Maycomb Tribune.

Dolphus Raymond—*A white man who lives with blacks.*

Judge Taylor—*The judge who presides at Tom Robinson's trial.*

Mrs. Grace Merriweather, Mrs. Gertrude Farrow, Mrs. Perkins, Mrs. Gates—*Members of the missionary circle.*

Sarah and Frances Barber (also known as Tutti and Frutti)—*Two deaf sisters.*

Summary of the Novel

Two plots run through the book *To Kill a Mockingbird*. The first is the mystery of the Radley Place and its inhabitant Boo Radley. The children work throughout the first part of the novel to bring him out or to see him inside the house.

The second plot is that of the accusation of Thomas Robinson as a rapist, his trial, and his conviction. Even though Tom is convicted, Mr. Robert Ewell and Mayella are not believed; Robert Ewell is determined to seek revenge on Atticus.

When Bob Ewell seeks to kill Jem and Scout, Boo Radley hears the commotion and manages to kill Ewell before he can harm the children further. The sheriff refuses to tell the story of Boo Radley to the community; he protects him and his privacy.

Estimated Reading Time

The total reading time for the 281-page book should be about $9\frac{1}{2}$ hours. Reading the book according to the natural chapter breaks is the best approach.

To Kill a Mockingbird

Chapter 1

New Characters:

Atticus Finch: *a Southern lawyer and the father of Scout and Jem*

Scout: *the six-year-old daugher of Atticus and the innocent narrator of* To Kill a Mockingbird

Dill: *a six-year-old summer visitor to Maycomb and a friend of both Scout and Jem*

The Radley Family: *Mr. and Mrs. Radley and their sons, Arthur and Nathan, who are the antagonists for the first 11 chapters of the novel*

Jem: *the ten-year-old son of Atticus and the brother of Scout*

Miss Stephanie Crawford: *the neighborhood gossip, a woman in her late sixties who has never been married*

Calpurnia: *the cook for the Finch family*

Miss Rachel Haverford: *Dill's aunt with whom Dill is spending the summer*

Summary

Scout is the narrator of and a main protagonist in *To Kill a Mockingbird.* Scout's real name is Jean Louise Finch, and she is the only daughter of Atticus Finch. She is a very precocious child, but she still has an air of innocence about her. In Chapter 1 she is six, but she is recalling the events of the novel from a later time in her life.

Ten-year-old Jem is the only son of Atticus Finch. Jem was six when his mother died and Scout believes he still misses her badly; but since Jem is at times secretive, Scout cannot be sure. Scout says she reckons time from when 13-year-old Jem broke his arm, but she does not give the complete details. To find out more about this event, one must read further.

Calpurnia, the cook for the Finch family, is described through Scout's eyes as "a tyrannical presence as long as I can remember." Scout explains that Calpurnia calls her home before she is ready to come and is always supported by Atticus. The children call Calpurnia and Atticus by their first names; they address all other adults with a title.

Charles Baker Harris—better known as Dill—is the nephew of Miss Rachel Haverford, the next-door neighbor of the Finch family. In Chapter 1 Dill is seven when he comes from Meridian, Mississippi, for his first summer visit in Maycomb. Dill is described by Scout as a "pocket Merlin, whose head teemed with eccentric plans,

strange longings, and quaint fancies." It is Dill who challenges the others to help draw Boo from his home.

The Radley family—Mr. and Mrs. Radley, their older son Nathan, and "Boo," lives next door to the Finch family. The Radley family, which is headed now by Nathan, is a very aloof one. Mr. Radley is described by Miss Stephanie Crawford as being "...so upright he took the word of God as his only law...." When Boo breaks the law and resists arrest as a teenager, Mr. Radley no longer allows him out of the house; even the death of Mr. Radley cannot free Boo, because Nathan assumes his father's role.

Miss Stephanie Crawford is the "neighborhood scold." It is from her that Scout is able to find out most of the information about the Radley family—including the fact that Boo stabbed his father in the leg. Miss Stephanie even declares that Boo looked straight through her window one night.

Analysis

Chapter 1 sets the stage for *To Kill a Mockingbird.* It introduces the characters who live on the main residential street in Maycomb and lets Dill and the reader know of the mystery surrounding the Radley Place. The reader finds out that Boo has been inside his home for years. Through Miss Stephanie the children have learned how Boo ran with the wrong crowd when he was a teenager. On one occasion Boo and his friends drove backwards around the courthouse square and resisted arrest. Mr. Radley asked to handle the matter himself, promising that his son would give no further trouble. He confined his son to the house where he became a recluse. According to local gossip, the next time Boo was seen or heard was the day he stabbed his father in the leg with a pair of scissors while cutting items from the newspaper for his scrapbook. Mr. Radley ran screaming into the street, and the sheriff locked Boo in the courthouse basement. After a short while he was returned to the Radley home and was never heard from again. When Mr. Radley dies, Nathan moves back home to take charge. Dill is fascinated with the story and determined to draw out Boo Radley.

As we learn the story of the Radley family, we also learn of certain conflicts between and even within the characters of *To Kill a Mockingbird.*

The children, provoked by their curiosity about the reclusive Boo Radley, concentrate on learning as much as possible about him. They spend the long, slow summer days thinking of ways to catch a glimpse of him. As they become caught up in the stories and superstitions surrounding him, they seem to lose sight of him as a person and think of him instead as a ghost or a hidden spectacle. They even use him to compete with each other, as they try to prove who can get closest to him and who is least afraid of him.

Throughout the book characters struggle to overcome inner fears, and in Chapter 1, we encounter a childish version of this. For the children, approaching Boo's house despite their fear is a thrill or a game. Later in the novel characters acting despite their fear will have much more serious results.

The Radley family, in cutting itself off from society, also forms a pattern that will become more important later in the novel. All of the many kinds of people in Maycomb fit together to form an intricate social balance. When a family becomes cut off from this, they seem to have trouble surviving on their own.

Harper Lee (through Scout's narration) uses many stylistic devices in Chapter 1. Scout uses *personification,* which is the representation of a thing, quality, or idea as a person. She does this when she describes the picket fence at the Radley Place as drunkenly guarding the yard and when she states that "pecan trees shook their fruit...." Lee uses *simile* when she likens one thing to another through the use of the words *as* and *like.* For instance, Scout says that the Radley Place drew Dill "...as the moon draws water" and that "...by nightfall the ladies were like soft teacakes with frostings of sweat and sweet talcum." Scout uses a *metaphor* when she calls one thing something else. For example, she says that the Radley home is occupied by a "malevolent phantom." *Humor* is another stylistic device employed. For instance, when Miss Stephanie describes Mr. Radley as being "so upright that he took the word of God as his only law," Scout does not understand and agrees that Mr. Radley's posture was indeed "ramrod straight."

Scout uses excellent grammar and has an extensive vocabulary for her age. The characters she quotes, however, often use the everyday speech or Southern *dialect* of the 1930s. For instance, a reference is made twice in Chapter 1 to the occupation of buying cotton, which Scout explains is "a polite term for doing nothing."; another time Jem tells Dill, "You look right puny for goin' on seven."

The plot order employs *flashback*, an interruption in the continuity of a story by the narration of an earlier episode. Scout begins by saying, "When he was nearly thirteen, my brother Jem got his arm badly broken at the elbow." She then states that, "When enough years had gone by to enable us to look back on them, we sometimes discussed the events leading to the accident." Lee then uses flashback when she refers to the days of Andrew Jackson.

Dill serves an important role in *To Kill a Mockingbird.* Upon his arrival, Scout tells him about Maycomb, the Radleys, and some of the other residents of the town. Through Dill's introduction, the reader can meet the characters and tour Scout's and Jem's territory—the boundaries of which have been set by Calpurnia's calling voice.

The education of Scout and Jem is a major theme running throughout *To Kill a Mockingbird.* In Chapter 1 Atticus teaches two lessons. First, he tells the children to mind their "own business and let the Radleys mind theirs, they had a right too..." His second lesson to the children is that there are many ways "of making people into ghosts." The children, however, do not immediately understand.

This idea of ghosts, superstitions, and the sober, haunted atmosphere of the Radley Place is a secondary theme which permeates Chapter 1 and appears in other chapters throughout the book.

Bravery versus cowardice is another theme that appears in the chapter. Scout states that Jem passed the Radley Place "always running" and that, "A Negro would not pass the Radley Place at night...." Dill's aunt locks up tight at night because of her fear of Arthur. Dill dares Jem to touch the house and contrasts the bravery of the folks in Meridian with the cowardliness of the people in Maycomb.

The chapter ends with a sense of foreboding; the last words are that the Radley "house was still."

Study Questions

1. Describe Calpurnia as Scout depicts her in Chapter 1.

2. What does Dill dare Jem to do?

3. What events led to Arthur's being shut into the house?

4. Pretend you are writing a description of Maycomb for a travel magazine of the 1930s. Describe the town in detail.

5. The townspeople of Maycomb have some fears and superstitions about the Radley Place. Describe these fears and superstitions.

6. Whose idea was it to make Boo come out of the house?

7. How important is bravery to Jem?

8. Mr. Connor is described as "Maycomb's ancient beadle." What is a *beadle*?

9. What goal do the children plan to achieve before the end of the summer?

10. Describe some of the customs of the town of Maycomb.

Answers

1. Calpurnia has been the cook for the Finch family since Jem was born. Scout describes Calpurnia as all angles and bones, nearsighted, and owning a wide, hard hand which she used to discipline Scout. Scout says Calpurnia is "always ordering me out of the kitchen, asking me why I couldn't behave as well as Jem…and calling me home when I wasn't ready to come."

2. Dill dares Jem to touch the Radley house.

3. Arthur and some other boys formed a group which was the nearest thing that Maycomb had ever had to a gang. They hung around the barbershop, rode the bus on Sundays to go to the movies, attended dances at the "gambling hell," and experimented with whiskey.

4. Maycomb is a small Southern town where the residents all know one another. The citizens are primarily law-abiding

people. The class system is in effect and there is segregation evidenced by the statement that the sheriff hadn't the heart to put Arthur in "jail alongside Negroes."

5. The people of Maycomb say that Arthur goes out at night after the town is asleep. Many people fear the Radley Place and cross the street to avoid it. Any lost ball in the Radley's yard remains there.

6. It was Dill's idea to make Boo come out of his house.

7. Scout says that Jem always takes a dare. Bravery is of great importance to him. It is because of his need to be brave that Jem runs into the Radley yard and slaps the house.

8. A beadle is a crier or officer of the court. Mr. Connor is evidently a bailiff of the court.

9. Before the end of the summer the children run out of ideas for play. Dill gives them the idea to make Boo Radley come out of his house.

10. On Sundays the people of Maycomb go visiting; the ladies wear their Sunday best for this event. The Radleys do not participate, however; they keep their shades drawn to discourage visitors. The pace on Sundays in Maycomb is slow; the citizens scorn activities like picture shows on Sundays.

When serious illness comes to a family, sawhorses are put up to cut down on traffic and noise. Straw is put in the street to cut down the noise of those who must use the street. The primary social events in the town are church-related activities.

Suggested Essay Topics

1. Describe Boo Radley, through the eyes of Jem and Scout Finch. Discuss his habits, his appearance, and his actions.

2. After defining the words "Caste" and "Class," describe the caste and class system in Maycomb. Do you think such a system would still exist in the town today? Why, or why not?

Chapter 2

New Characters:

Miss Caroline: *the new first-grade teacher and Scout's antagonist*

Walter Cunningham: *a poor but proud member of the Cunningham family and Scout's classmate*

Summary

Chapter 2 describes Scout's first day in school. The new teacher, Miss Caroline Fisher, spanks Scout's hand before the morning is over. The conflict between Scout and Miss Fisher begins when Miss Fisher finds out that Scout can read; Miss Fisher tells Scout not to allow her father to teach her anymore. Scout says that her father did not teach her to read and proceeds to tell Miss Fisher of Jem's belief that Scout was swapped at birth and that she was born reading *The Mobile Register*. Miss Fisher closes the conversation by saying that Atticus does not know how to teach.

Miss Fisher next comes in conflict with Walter Cunningham. She tries to get him to take a quarter to buy his lunch. Scout explains that Walter is a Cunningham who will not take "anything off of anybody," but Miss Fisher will not listen and spanks her hand. The class does not understand what has happened at first, but when they realize that Scout has been whipped, they begin to laugh. Miss Blount, the sixth-grade teacher, threatens the whole first-grade class because her class cannot concentrate with all the noise in Scout's class.

As the morning—and the chapter—end, Scout leaves for her lunch and sees Miss Fisher crying. Scout concludes by thinking, "Had her conduct been more friendly toward me, I would have felt sorry for her."

Analysis

There is a conflict between Scout and Miss Caroline when the new teacher discovers that Scout can read. She shames Scout by saying that Atticus should not teach her anymore because he does not know how to teach. Miss Caroline vows to undo the damage Atticus has done with his teaching.

Miss Caroline proves her insensitivity once again in a conflict with Walter Cunningham. When Miss Caroline inspects the children's lunches and finds Walter Cunningham does not have one, she tries to lend Walter money. Walter will not accept the loan. Although he is poor, he is proud. The conflict is heightened when Scout tries to explain about the Cunninghams and about Maycomb society to the new teacher, but the teacher—unlike Dill—is unwilling to listen. Miss Caroline tells Jean Louise that she has had enough of her, spanks her hand with a ruler, and threatens the class. The conflict reaches a climax when the sixth-grade teacher comes in

and personally reprimands the whole class because they are too noisy.

In Chapter 2, Scout struggles with herself to stay quiet when she realizes she has annoyed her teacher. Later on, however, she abandons her resolve and tries to explain things to Miss Caroline. Scout has difficulty with her words; she wants to explain the Cunninghams' view as Atticus would have done, but she realizes it is beyond her ability.

Miss Caroline's ignorance about the workings of Maycomb prove once again how intricately the society is constructed. Even the Cunningham's poverty is part of this system. Miss Caroline, a stranger to this system, does not understand it, and causes chaos in the classroom when she tries to interfere with it. She does not recognize that Scout is trying to show her how it works.

In Chapter 2 Harper Lee continues to employ stylistic devices in her writing. *Foreshadowing*, or a hint as to what is to come, is employed when Scout, in her narration, tells the reader that before "the first morning was over, Miss Caroline Fisher, our teacher, hauled me up to the front of the room and patted the palm of my hand with a rule, then made me stand in the corner until noon." The reader is unsure why this happens and wants to read more. The statement also gives the reader a hint that more unpleasantness may be in store for Scout in the afternoon.

The reader is hooked by the second chapter and must continue to explore the *progressive plot* to find out the answers to the many unanswered questions.

Harper continues to use *simile*. For instance, Scout says that her new teacher looks and smells "like a peppermint drop." The *humor* used by Scout in describing her first day helps the reader to endure with her the shame and mortification brought about by public education. For example, when the teacher asks if the students recognize the alphabet, the narrator (Scout) tells the reader that most of the students did; they had encountered them last year—their first year in first grade.

Scout does not recognize Jem's *malapropism*, a ridiculous misuse of words. The new teacher is using the Language Experience Approach of Experiential Learning; John Dewey, a prominent educator of the time, advocates this method. Jem, however, mistakenly refers to the method as the Dewey Decimal System, a system of cataloging library materials. Scout also believes Jem when he attempts to explain the meaning of the word *entailment*, Jem tells her it is "a condition of having your tail in a crack." These errors, however, serve to add *humor* to the chapter.

Scout continues to give examples of the 1930s Southern *dialect* in the speech of Walter Cunningham. At one time Walter responds to his teacher by saying, "Nome thank you ma'am." Another time he mumbles "Yeb'm."

Harper continues to use *flashback*. For example, Scout begins, "My special knowledge of the Cunningham tribe...was gained from events of last winter." Scout proceeds to explain the situation that gave her this information.

Lee also uses *irony*, an action which is unexpected or contrary to what one would expect. Miss Caroline says she uses experiential learning yet she tells Scout not to read at home. It is ironic that Miss Caroline tries to curb Scout's experiences with reading when she purports to teach through the use of experiences. The irony is increased when Miss Caroline tells Scout that her father does not know how to teach; since Scout is reading easily and well, Atticus evidently does know how to teach.

Through Scout's explanations of Maycomb society to the new teacher (and to Dill in Chapter 1), the reader is apprised of the intricacies of the Alabama town. The reader, unlike Miss Caroline, is able to profit from the information presented to the new teacher.

The *motif* of education is continued in Chapter 2. The reader is made aware of the sharp contrast between Atticus's methods of instruction and those of the new teacher. The patience of Atticus is opposed to the impatience of Miss Caroline. The corporal punishment used by Miss Caroline is quite different from the gentle reasoning employed by Atticus. Scout learned to read at home by experiential learning: she sat on Atticus's lap and watched his moving finger as he read. Miss Caroline, however, forbids her to read anymore at home.

Bravery versus cowardice is found again in this chapter. Scout, though aware of the possible consequences, still comes to the aid of Walter, her classmate—a good example of bravery. When the teacher herself is faced with opposition in the form of Miss Blount, she buckles under the pressure. It is Scout who shows bravery and the teacher who shows cowardliness.

Study Questions

1. Who is Scout's first grade teacher?

2. What is the Dewey Decimal System?

3. What events lead to the conflict between Scout and Miss Caroline?

4. Why is Mrs. Blount, the sixth-grade teacher, angry with Miss Caroline?

5. How does Scout learn to read?

6. The students in the class show some prejudice against Miss Caroline when she tells the class she is from Winston County, Alabama. Explain this prejudice.

7. How does Miss Caroline contradict herself about the use of imagination?

8. How does Miss Caroline contradict herself in her views on teaching reading?

9. How does Scout learn to write?

10. Describe the Cunningham family.

Answers

1. Miss Caroline is Scout's first-grade teacher.

2. The Dewey Decimal System is a way of arranging library books and materials. It is not a way to teach reading, as Jem mistakenly explains.

3. Scout finds disfavor with Miss Caroline, first of all, when she reads aloud from *The Mobile Register* and from *My First Reader*. Later, when Scout tries to explain the Cunningham philosophy, she angers Miss Caroline even more.

4. Miss Blount says the sixth grade cannot concentrate on their study of the pyramids because of the noise in the first-grade

class. She is angry with Miss Caroline Fisher for allowing—and possibly contributing to—the chaos.

5. Scout learns to read by climbing into Atticus's lap and watching his finger move underneath the print of whatever he might be reading.

6. Miss Caroline is from North Alabama, from Winston County. On January 11, 1861, when Alabama seceded from the Union, Winston County did not condone this action; it seceded from Alabama. The rest of the state was still angry with Winston County 70 years later. In addition, the rest of the state believed that the county "was full of Liquor Interests, Big Mules, steel companies, Republicans, professors, and other persons of no background."

7. Miss Caroline reads a very imaginative story to the students about chocolate malted mice and cats with clothes. The farm children are not at all impressed with the story. Later when Scout is telling about a change in her family name, Miss Caroline will not listen. Miss Caroline admonishes Scout; "Let's not let our imaginations run away with us, dear…"

8. Miss Caroline says that Atticus "does not know how to teach"; yet Scout is reading well—even the stock-market quotations. She tells Scout that "It's best to begin reading with a fresh mind." Scout, however, is not a beginning reader but a good one. Miss Caroline advocates the Language Experience Approach which uses sight words on cards; she does not advocate the phonics method which uses the alphabet and has the students sound out words. Scout seems to know the letters and is reading by that method, but Miss Caroline wants to change her way of reading.

9. Scout learns to write at the kitchen table with Calpurnia setting her a writing task. Calpurnia would write the alphabet across the top of a tablet and then copy a Bible chapter beneath. Scout's task would be to copy the material satisfactorily. A reward of a bread, butter, and sugar sandwich would be doled out if Calpurnia considered the task well-done.

10. The Cunningham family is a poor family. They are so poor

that Scout believes that Walter "had probably never seen three quarters together at the same time in his life." Despite the lack of material possessions, the Cunninghams have a reputation to uphold. They never take anything they cannot pay back. They even refuse church baskets and scrip stamps. The family does not have much, but they get along with what they have. When they use Atticus' services, they pay him back with stovewood, hickory nuts, smilax, holly, and turnip greens. The Cunninghams have pride in their land and go hungry to keep it and to vote as they please.

Suggested Essay Topics

1. Contrast the teaching styles of Atticus Finch and Miss Caroline Fisher.

2. Describe the outward appearance and the actions of Miss Caroline. Are there any contradictions between the two?

Chapter 3

New Characters:

Little Chuck Little: *Scout's polite, brave classmate*

Burris Ewell: *Scout's surly classmate who attends school once a year*

Summary

Chapter 3 occurs over a six-hour period from lunchtime until nightfall of Scout's first day in school. Scout takes out her frustration with school and especially with Miss Caroline by rubbing Walter's nose in the dirt of the school yard as the lunch break begins. Jem stops the slaughter and Scout quickly explains that Walter made her start school "on the wrong foot." Jem serves as a peacemaker and invites Walter to their home for lunch. Scout pledges not to fight him again.

On the way home, the three pass the Radley Place and a discussion of the fears and superstitions associated with the house ensues. Walter remembers eating pecans supposedly poisoned by Boo Radley and recalls how sick he was.

At home Atticus accepts Walter as an equal; there is no class differentiation in the Finch home. During lunch Calpurnia disciplines Scout for commenting on the way that Walter pours syrup on his food. Even though it means walking past the Radley Place alone on her way back to school, Scout remains behind to advise "Atticus on Calpurnia's inequities." Atticus, however, only reminds Scout of the trouble she causes Calpurnia who works so hard for her. Atticus refuses to fire the cook as Scout suggests.

A new conflict develops in the afternoon between the teacher and Burris Ewell, another student. Miss Caroline sees a louse on Burris and becomes hysterical. Little Chuck Little tries to smooth things out. When Miss Caroline asks Burris to sit down, he becomes angry. Little Chuck Little tells Miss Caroline to "Let him go ma'am…He's a mean one…and there's some little folks here." Scout describes how Little Chuck Little's hand goes to his pocket and he threatens Burris with "I'd soon's kill you as look at you. Now go home."

The end result is that Burris hurls insults at Miss Caroline and leaves the class. Miss Caroline cries but she manages to recover and tell the class a story about a toad and a hall, probably *Wind in the Willows*.

That night Calpurnia surprises Scout with crackling bread. After supper Scout asks Atticus if she can leave school like Burris, but Atticus says that she must obey the law. He tries to teach Scout a lesson about walking around in another person's skin. Atticus and Scout do reach one compromise: if she will go to school, they will continue reading at night. As an aside, he asks her not to mention their reading at school.

Analysis

Although every member of the Finch family understands the way Maycomb society works, they do not conform to Maycomb's rules of class. Walter is welcomed into the home by Atticus. The Ewell family, on the other hand, in no way fits into Maycomb society. They even live on the edge of town. Burris and his father refuse to obey the school attendance rules and the hunting regulations of Maycomb. Society elects to turn a blind eye on these activities.

Scout learns several lessons in Chapter 3. Calpurnia teaches Scout that when people differ, Scout is not "called on to contradict 'em...." Scout also learns from Calpurnia that guests in her home should be treated as such. Atticus teachers her to consider things from another person's point of view in order to understand that person. He indicates that sometimes it is better to bend the law a little in special cases. He also tells Scout that at times it is best to ignore things. He reminds her that Maycomb overlooks Burris's skipping school and Robert Ewell's hunting out of season. He applies this to Jem in the tree house; if Scout will ignore Jem, Jem will come down.

Harper Lee continues to use may stylistic devices in Chapter 3. The repetition of sounds, or *alliteration*, is used often. For instance, the reader finds words like "snorted and slouched" and "snot-nosed slut." Scout uses an *idiom* when she says that Walter made her start off "on the wrong foot." Walter's *dialect* is apparent as he says, "Almost died first year I come to school and et them pecans—folks say he pizened 'em and put 'em over on the school side of the fence."

Once again the children must prove their bravery in the face of many threats. Often, this is easier in a group. The children walk by the Radley Place when they are together, but go by "at a full gallop" when they are alone. The children fake bravado in front of their peers, but they allow free rein to their feelings when they are unobserved. Bravery versus cowardice also occurs with the confrontation of Little Chuck Little and Burris in the classroom. Little Chuck Little, one of the smallest children in the class, displays bravery and is able to confront Burris, "...a hard-down mean one."

Study Questions

1. Describe Burris Ewell.

2. Little Chuck Little tells the teacher that Mr. Ewell is "right contentious." What does this mean?

3. What events lead to Burris's leaving school before the day is over?

4. Why does Atticus say that Scout is not to mention the compromise they made when she goes to school?

5. What is a cootie?

6. Why does Walter think he almost died the first year in school?

7. Why does Atticus say Scout should ignore Jem in the tree house?

8. When Walter gets near the Finch house, Scout says he "had forgotten he was a Cunningham." What does she mean?

9. What does it mean to "climb into his skin and walk around in it?"

10. Tell what a compromise is and give an example.

Answers

1. Burris was the filthiest human Scout had ever seen. His neck was dark grey and his nails were black into the quick. He was

rude to the teacher and said that she could not make him
do anything he did not want to do.

2. He meant that Mr. Ewell was quarrelsome.

3. First, Miss Caroline saw a "cootie" on him. Then she dis-
    missed him for the rest of the day to go home and wash his
    hair in lye soap and kerosene; she also reminded him—in
    front of the class—to bathe before coming back to school.
    After he tells her he will not be back, she asks him to sit down.
    Burris refuses and is confronted by Chuck. Miss Caroline tells
    him to go home or she will get the principal. Burris reminds
    her impolitely that she cannot make him do anything. He
    waits until he is sure she is crying, and then he shuffles off
    home. Burris always quits school the first day.

4. Atticus says at first that the learned authorities would receive
    their activities with "considerable disapprobation," or dis-
    approval. He translates it to mean that he does not want Miss
    Caroline after him.

5. A cootie is another name for a head or body louse.

6. Walter thinks he almost died from eating poisoned pecans.

7. He tells her one should ignore some things. This is a type of
    behavior modification.

8. Walter has quickly forgotten that the Cunninghams do not
    accept that which they cannot repay. He is eager to eat!

9. Atticus is merely trying to get Scout to put herself in some-
    one else's position.

10. A compromise is an agreement reached by two parties; of-
    ten some concessions must be made by one or both of the
    parties. An example from *To Kill a Mockingbird* is when
    Atticus and Scout decide to continue to read each night if
    Scout will go to school.

Suggested Essay Topics

1. Contrast Atticus Finch's idea of the law and Mr. Radley's idea
    of the law.

2. Compare and contrast Walter Cunningham and Burris Ewell.

Chapter 4

New Characters:

Mrs. Henry Lafayette Dubose: *"the meanest old woman who ever lived"*

Cecil Jacobs: *one of Scout's classmates*

Summary

Scout's first-grade year finally ends; her conclusion is that she has been cheated out of something. Each day she runs by the Radley Place 30 minutes before Jem. One day she finds gum in the

tree near the Radley home. When she tells Jem about the gum, he makes her spit it out. On the last day of school the two children walk home together. They find a package covered with foil and containing two scrubbed, Indian-head pennies in the tree near the Radley Place. The children cannot figure out the source of the treasures.

When Dill arrives for the summer, the children re-establish their friendship. Their conversations are centered around ghosts and superstitions.

On one of their first days of freedom, Jem gives Scout first push in the tire. Scout does not realize that Jem is angry with her until he pushes the tire with all the strength in his body. Dizzy and nauseated, Scout finds herself in front of the Radley house. Hearing the two boys scream loudly, Scout runs for her life and leaves the tire behind. It is Jem who finally retrieves the tire.

Dill invents a new game: Boo Radley. The children dramatize Boo's story from the bits of gossip and legend they have heard and from their own additions. If Mr. Nathan passes by, they immediately stand still and silent. One day when they are involved in the game, they fail to see Atticus approach. He asks them what they are doing, but Jem replies, "Nothing." Atticus takes the scissors from them and asks them if the game has to do with the Radleys. Jem denies that it does and Atticus goes inside.

The children debate whether to continue the game. Because Scout does not want to, Jem complains that she is acting like a girl. Scout reminds them that she believes Atticus knows about the game. She keeps to herself her second reason for wanting to quit the game: laughter she heard when the tire landed near the Radley house.

Analysis

In Chapter 4, the children still regard the Radley family with childish fascination. They act out their visions of the Radleys in much the same way they had previously acted out stories they had read. This shows that they regard the family as almost fictional. They give little thought to the fact that their game may be hurtful to thinking, feeling humans behind the Radley windows. In his quiet way, Atticus tries to teach them about this. Later in the novel

Atticus will try to teach a similar lesson to the inhabitants of Maycomb during the trial of Tom Robinson.

It is a good thing that Atticus is such a good teacher, because Scout is sorely disappointed with the formal education she is receiving. It seems to her that the school system, an arm of society, is devised to keep her from learning. This causes Scout to believe that she "was being cheated out of something."

Fears and superstitions associated with the Radley Place comprise an important theme in this chapter. To further intrigue the reader, Harper Lee uses *foreshadowing* with the quotation, "There was more to it than he knew, but I decided not to tell him." Chapter 4 is a *cliffhanger;* the open ending of the chapter is the sentence "Someone inside the house was laughing."

Imagery is the predominant stylistic device employed in Chapter 4. Through the effective descriptions of Harper Lee, the reader is able to visualize Jem retrieving the tire. "Jem…ran down the sidewalk, treaded water at the gate, then dashed in and retrieved the tire," is countered with the equally strong image of "Atticus standing on the sidewalk looking at us, slapping a rolled newspaper against his knee."

Bravery versus cowardice (a secondary theme) is found throughout the chapter. The reader finds Scout running past the Radley Place in fear each day since she must go home alone from school; on the last day of school Jem and Scout walk together, rather than run, past the gloomy house. Later Jem conquers his fear long enough to go into the yard of the Radley Place to retrieve the tire while Dill and Scout look on at the performance. Bravery seems to occur when there are others watching rather than when the children are alone.

Study Questions

1. What is the first present Scout finds in the tree?

2. When Dill says that he helped engineer the train, Jem says, "In a pig's ear you did, Dill." What does this mean?

3. Why has "Calpurnia's tyranny, unfairness, and meddling… faded to gentle grumblings of general disapproval," according to Scout?

4. What does Jem call Miss Caroline's teaching methods?

5. What is the second present found in the tree?

6. Who is the "meanest old woman that ever lived"?

7. When Atticus asks the children if their game pertains to the Radleys, Jem says "No sir." Atticus merely responds, "I hope it doesn't." Why does he stop the conversation at that point?

8. How do cowardice and bravery figure into Scout's taking part in the dramas about the Radley family?

9. What is the meaning of the following: "Dill was a villain's villain..."?

10. What is a Hot Steam?

Answers

1. Scout finds chewing gum in the tree first.

2. The idiomatic expression "In a pig's ear" means "impossible."

3. Scout's attitude—rather than Calpurnia's behavior—may be the reason for the statement. Scout is spending less time with Calpurnia; possibly they miss each other. Scout is also growing and maturing; this is probably a principal reason for their improved relationship. Scout herself admits that she "went to much trouble, sometimes, not to provoke her."

4. He calls it the Dewey Decimal System.

5. Indian-head pennies are the second gifts found in the tree.

6. Mrs. Henry Lafayette Dubose is the "meanest old woman that ever lived."

7. Atticus may have been following his own lesson: ignore the behavior and it will go away. Atticus did not usually forbid the children to do anything. Rather he posed things in such a way that they could make their own decision.

8. Scout is at first frightened to participate in the dramas. Jem and Dill accuse her of being afraid. After the incident with Atticus, Scout is hesitant about playing again. Jem accuses her of "being a girl."

9. The statement "Dill was a villain's villain" means that Dill is good in the role; he can play a villain to the degree that even a real villain would be pleased with the performance.

10. A Hot Steam can be detected if one is walking along a lonesome road at night and comes to a hot place. The Hot Steam is actually someone who cannot get into heaven and just stays in lonely places. If a person walks through the Hot Steam, the person will become Hot Steam after death and perhaps even suck the breath from people.

Suggested Essay Topics

1. What evidence does one have that Boo Radley is trying to make friends with the children?

2. How is Scout growing and maturing as the story progresses?

Chapter 5

New Characters:

Miss Maudie Atkinson: *the neighbor who had grown up with Jack Finch*

Uncle Jack Finch: *Atticus's doctor-brother, ten years his junior*

Summary

Scout begins to spend more time with Miss Maudie. The two talk about religion and anything else Scout wants to discuss. Miss Maudie treats Scout as an equal. She tells Scout to call Boo Radley by his real name: Arthur Radley, and she believes that Arthur does not come out of the house because he wants to stay inside. When Scout tells her that Jem believes he has died and been stuck up the chimney, Miss Maudie compares Jem to his Uncle Jack. It is apparent that Maudie and Atticus have similar views about the rights and dignity of the Radleys and of all people.

Jem and Dill (with Scout looking on) try to send a message to Boo by tying it on a fishing pole and casting it toward his window. Because Dill fails to ring the bell which he is to use at the first sign of anyone approaching, Atticus catches them. Atticus gives them several rules to obey: They are not to play the game he had seen them playing, make fun of others, or go to the Radley Place unless they are invited.

Jem is silent until Atticus is out of hearing. Then he yells that he is not sure that he wants to be a lawyer.

Analysis

Once again, in this chapter, we see how an individual who separates himself from society can become a spectacle for those who fit in. Furthermore, we see again that Atticus, though he himself is a member of society, does not chastise others for choosing not to be. He tries to understand why they choose to remain apart. Boo Radley continues to be a recluse and continues to arouse the curiosity of Maycomb. Atticus, however, does not condemn Arthur for living alone. He reminds the children that "What Mr. Radley does is his own business." Miss Maudie, also, reminds Scout that Arthur Radley is a human being despite the rumors spread about him.

She says that he deserves to be left alone if he prefers. Their attitudes are not typical of the rest of Maycomb society which continues to condemn and whisper about Arthur.

To Kill a Mockingbird is a *novel of maturation.* The reader sees the growth and the coming maturity of Scout, Jem, and Dill. Chapter 5 emphasizes, however, that though Scout has grown, she still has innocence. For instance, when Miss Stephanie accuses Arthur Radley of looking in her window, Miss Maudie loudly asks Miss Stephanie if she moved over in bed for him. Scout misses the sexual implication and thinks it is Miss Maudie's loud voice that shuts Miss Stephanie up for a while.

In Chapter 5 Harper Lee continues to stress the *motif* of fears and superstitions associated with the Radley Place. Scout discusses her fears and superstitions with Miss Maudie. Miss Maudie reflects that the stories about Arthur are "…three-fourths colored folks and one-fourth Stephanie Crawford." If Maycomb society cannot get him to conform, they will make him what they will through their stories. When the curious and frightened children try to deliver a note to Arthur and are caught by Atticus, they are given certain rules to follow—another evidence of the *education motif* that pervades *To Kill a Mockingbird.*

In this chapter, once again, the Radley Place serves as a challenge for the children, a chance for them to prove who is brave and who is cowardly. Scout admits to feeling terror just thinking of delivering a note to Boo Radley, but she suggests that Jem "…just knock the front door down…." Jem uses a pole to try to deliver a message to Boo; this shows his bravery is limited. Jem does not talk back to Atticus until he is out of earshot—a concession of cowardliness to the others who observe him. Who is brave and who is cowardly has not yet been established.

Study Questions

1. When Scout begins to drift away from the boys, with whom does she spend much time?

2. Why does Miss Maudie hate her house?

3. Why do the children have faith in Miss Maudie?

4. How do the children try to send the message to Boo?

5. What does Miss Maudie mean when she says Atticus is the same in his house as he is on the public streets?

6. What does Uncle Jack yell at Miss Maudie each Christmas?

7. Atticus uses something like a threat when he finds the children trying to get a note to Boo Radley. What is the threat?

8. Uncle Jack Finch says the "best defense to her [Miss Maudie] was spirited offense." What does he mean by that?

9. What does Miss Maudie mean when she says that the things told about Arthur Radley are "three-fourths colored folks and one-fourth Stephanie Crawford"?

10. What gesture of friendship cements Miss Maudie's and Scout's relationship?

Answers

1. Scout begins to spend time with Miss Maudie Atkinson.

2. She considers time spent indoors time wasted. She prefers to spend as much time as possible working in her garden.

3. She has never told on them; she has always been honest with them; she does not pry.

4. The children try to send a message by tying it on a fishing line.

5. She means that Atticus is a man of integrity; the face he presents in public does not differ from the face he presents at home.

6. He yells for Miss Maudie to come out and marry him.

7. He threatens Jem with the possibility that Jem may not become a lawyer.

8. Jack means that he would tease Miss Maudie before she could tease him.

9. She means that most of the things told about Arthur are superstition and gossip.

10. Miss Maudie pushes out her false teeth for Scout to see.

Suggested Essay Topics

1. Explain why Miss Maudie Atkinson would be a good friend for a young, motherless girl to have.

2. What lessons did Atticus Finch try to teach the children when he found them using a fishing line to give a message to Arthur Radley?

Chapter 6

New Character:

Mr. Avery: *a neighbor who boards across the street from Mrs. Dubose*

Summary

On Dill's last night in town for the summer, Jem and Dill decide to peep in the window at the Radley Place to see if they can see Boo. Scout comes along. A shadow appears and the children run in fear. When shots ring out, Jem leaves his pants caught on the barbed-wire fence. The children join the other Maycomb residents who have come out into the night to see what has happened. Later in the night Jem and Scout return to the Radley Place for Jem's pants.

Analysis

The children have violated the trust of the adults in their lives. The only way they can explain Jem's missing trousers is to lie. Dill says that they were playing strip poker. Scout and Jem fear losing the respect of Atticus, and Dill faces the anger of his Aunt Rachel. The judgment of the whole neighborhood is upon them when Jem appears in the crowd without pants and Dill tells his falsehood before the neighbors.

In Chapter 6, for the first time, the children must face their fear of the Radley Place for a more serious reason than to prove their bravery to one another. The danger that Jem faces in retrieving his trousers is no longer ghostly and insubstantial, and in a sense, his bravery is more real as well. This chapter includes a major departure: Jem is the only one of the children to show bravery near the

Radley Place even though he is not being observed by others. The reader will find later that he resists for a while his urge to tell Scout something that happens on this errand.

For the first time a child elects to approach the Radley Place without the direct observation of a peer. Jem shows bravery in going to the fence at night. The opinion of his father is more important than anything which might happen to him there. He is beginning to prioritize values in his life.

To Kill a Mockingbird continues to be a novel of *maturation,* or a *bildungsroman.* Although the reader has directly observed the growth and maturity of the narrator Scout, Chapter 6 emphasizes the maturity of Jem, her brother. When Jem insists that he must return for his pants despite his fears, Scout does not understand his compulsion. She recognizes that he is no longer following childish motivations. She admits, "It was then, I suppose, that Jem and I first begin to part company."

Study Questions

1. What is Mr. Avery's claim to fame?

2. What is the children's new plan in Chapter 6?

3. Where do the children sleep in the summer?

4. What are some of the nicknames that Jem gives Scout?

5. Why do the children spit on the gate?

6. How do you know that Jem respects his father?

7. What does Jem lose when he goes to the Radley Place?

8. What false story does Dill tell about the missing pants?

9. What promise/understanding exists between Scout and Dill?

10. How does Atticus take care of the poker problem?

Answers .

1. He can urinate "ten feet" into the yard.

2. The children develop a plan to look in on Arthur Radley.

3. The children often sleep on the porch in the summer.

4. Jem calls Scout "Angel May" and "Little Three-Eyes."

5. The children spit on the hinge to prevent it from squeaking.

6. The reader knows that Jem respects his father when he braves the Radley Place at night to retrieve his pants. Atticus has never spanked him, and Jem prefers to keep it that way.

7. Jem loses his pants when he goes to the Radley Place.

8. Dill says that the pants were lost in a game of strip poker.

9. They are engaged.

10. He tells the children to settle it themselves.

Suggested Essay Topics

1. Why did Jem return for his pants?

2. Why were the children going to spy on Arthur Radley on the last night of summer?

Chapter 7

Summary

Scout starts second grade. The children continue to look in the knothole and find presents: a ball of twine, two dolls carved from soap which resemble Jem and Scout, gum, a spelling medal, and a watch and pocketknife on a chain. Jem becomes very quiet. He finally tells Scout that the trousers he retrieved had been mended and neatly folded when he returned for them.

After Scout and Jem write a thank-you note and place it in the knothole, they return to find the knothole in the tree has been filled

with cement. Mr. Radley admits he filled up the hole, using the excuse that the tree was sick.

Jem seems to be spending a lot of time thinking. Scout believes that on one occasion he was crying as he watched the Radley Place.

Analysis

In Chapter 7 the children find themselves pitted against Nathan—not Arthur—Radley. When Nathan fills up the knothole where the children have been finding presents, they are devastated. Their fears and superstitions about Boo Radley are beginning to fade. Their conflict with Nathan Radley is more real to them now. This marks a passing of invented childish fears. Instead of battling ghosts, they are learning the complexities of communicating with real people, as an adult must.

Jem, especially, is showing signs of growing up. He becomes moody and private as he tries to absorb all that he is discovering about the real world. For quite some time he keeps a secret: the trousers he lost on the fence had been mended when he returned for them. Jem is struggling to control his emotions. When he goes by himself to cry the night after the knothole is filled in by Mr. Nathan Radley, it is not a childish display, but a sign that he is maturing.

Stylistic devices are evident in Chapter 7. Harper Lee makes use of many *hyperboles* (exaggerations) to express the feelings that Scout is experiencing. For instance, Scout remarks that "if I had gone alone to the Radley Place at two in the morning, my funeral would have been held the next afternoon." *Symbolism* is an important part of Chapter 7. Atticus continues to be the last word when any dispute arises. He is the *symbol* of stability in *To Kill a Mockingbird*. The tree is a symbol of Arthur Radley. Nathan fills the hole in the tree because "Tree's dying. You plug 'em with cement when they're sick." Atticus, however, acknowledges that the "…tree's as healthy as you are, Jem." Like the tree, Arthur, too, was treated by his family when he was not really sick. The tree, like Arthur, was a giver of gifts; Nathan prevented both from giving their gifts to others.

The bravery in Chapter 7 is that shown by the characters as they face everyday life—not ghosts and ghouls. Scout finds second grade is grim, but she endures and faces it each day with hope. Jem has told her that she will find things of value once she reaches sixth grade. Jem does not deny his feelings and expresses them—even to the point of crying when he is alone. He even bravely confronts Mr. Nathan Radley with his questions of why the tree was filled with cement.

Study Questions

1. What secret does Jem share with Scout?

2. Describe the typical seasons in South Alabama.

3. What is the difference between carving and whittling?

4. What was unusual about Jem's pants when he retrieved them from the fence?

5. What does Mr. Avery do with the stick of stovewood each week?

6. Why doesn't Miss Maudie chew gum?

7. What do the children leave in the knothole in the tree?

8. What does Mr. Nathan Radley do to the tree where the gifts are placed?

9. Atticus says the tree is healthy. Mr. Nathan Radley says it is sick. When Atticus is told that Nathan had said the tree was sick, what does Atticus say?

10. How does Jem respond to the tree being plugged with cement?

Answers

1. He says that when he returned for his pants, he found them patched and folded on the fence.

2. There is little change in the seasons. Winters are more like autumn than in other parts of the country.

3. Carving is to shape by cutting; whittling is just cutting without trying to make a shape.

4. When Jem retrieved the pants, they had been mended and folded.

5. Mr. Avery whittles the stick of stovewood down to a toothpick.

6. Miss Maudie does not chew gum because it stuck (cleaved) to her palate (the roof of her mouth).

7. Scout and Jem leave a thank-you note in the knothole in the tree.

8. Mr. Nathan fills the hole with cement.

9. He says that Nathan probably knows more about trees than he does.

10. Jem tells Scout not to cry, questions Mr. Nathan, goes to Atticus, and finally cries himself.

Suggested Essay Topics

1. What were the six gifts placed in the tree? Why do you think those gifts were chosen?

2. What are the children beginning to think of Boo as a person?

Chapter 8

New Character:

Eula May: *Maycomb's leading telephone operator*

Summary

Snow comes to Maycomb the day after Mrs. Radley's death. Eula May lets the Finch children know that school has been canceled. The children build a snow character by borrowing snow from Miss Maudie. They combine this snow with mud to make the figure, which at first resembles Mr. Avery and then is changed when Atticus protests.

That night Atticus wakes the children in the middle of the night and takes them outside. A fire is destroying Miss Maudie's house and the sparks are threatening the Finch home also.

At dawn Scout finds that someone has placed a blanket over her shoulders. Atticus tells her that the person was Arthur Radley. The next day Miss Maudie begins to make plans for her new home.

Analysis

In this chapter the children discover that most adults also have superstitious beliefs which they rely on to explain events that they don't understand. Mr. Avery blames the children for the bad weather since he thinks that children disobeying their parents, smoking, and making war on each other will cause the seasons to change. As residents of the town battle an unusual snow fall and later a fire which burns Miss Maudie's home, they try to find ways to explain these unnatural events. It is a common superstitious belief that unusual or unjust human actions can have repercussions on a natural level—causing disturbances or chaos.

The snowman (which later turns out to be a snow woman) is symbolic. It foreshadows events to come. The snowman is partly built with black Alabama soil. The colors—black, black and white, white, black again—foretell the racial unrest to occur later in the book. Chapter 9 will begin the development of a second plot involving Tom Robinson, Robert Ewell, and the court of law.

Scout's innocence is evident in this chapter. Scout misunderstands two words and Harper Lee derives much humor from this.

The two words Scout thinks she hears are "characterture" and "morphodite"; the words that are actually used are *caricature*, which is the deliberately distorted imitation of a person, and *hermaphrodite*, which means a being with the characteristics of both sexes.

Suspense is another sylistic device employed in Chapter 8. The reader waits with bated breath to find out what will happen during the fire.

Despite all the action in Chapter 8, lurking in the background is the theme of fears and superstitions associated with the Radleys and the Radley Place and the superstitions Mr. Avery associates with the actions of the children.

The whole neighborhood demonstrates bravery as they battle the blaze and wait in fear to find out if the fire will spread to their house.

Study Questions

1. Who dies in Chapter 8?

2. What is the Rosetta Stone? Why does Scout think Mr. Avery gets his information from it?

3. Why do Jem and Scout feel guilty when Mr. Avery tells them that children who disobey parents, smoke cigarettes, and make war on each other can cause a change in the seasons?

4. Jem and Scout do not have enough snow to build a snow figure. What else do they use?

5. What does Scout ask Atticus after he returns from the Radley Place after Mrs. Radley died?

6. Jem is able to make a snow person without enough snow to build one. What is Atticus's first reaction? His second reaction?

7. How is Miss Maudie able to take an interest in Jem and Scout when her house has just burned?

8. Before the children begin the snowman, what do they borrow from Miss Maudie?

9. Why does Jem not want Scout to walk in the snow or to eat it?

10. Why does Atticus take the children out of the house at 1:00 A.M.?

Answers

1. Mrs. Radley dies in Chapter 8.

2. The Rosetta Stone is a tablet of black basalt found in 1799 at Rosetta, Egypt. Because it has inscriptions in Greek and in ancient Egyptian characters, it is a key to deciphering the ancient Egyptian writing. Scout thinks Mr. Avery gets his outdated information from this stone.

3. Jem and Scout feel guilty because they were not perfect children and had at times disobeyed Atticus. Dill had rolled cigarettes at an earlier point in the book, so there is a possibility that Jem had smoked. The children had waged their own wars against others during the past year.

4. Scout and Jem combined the snow with mud from their own backyard.

5. When Atticus returns from the Radley Place, Scout asks if he had seen Arthur Radley.

6. Atticus praises Jem for the snow figure, but when he sees that it looks like Mr. Avery, he makes the children disguise it.

7. Miss Maudie is able to take an interest in Jem and Scout after her house burns because she values them more than her material possessions.

8. Before the children begin their snow person they borrow snow from Miss Maudie.

9. Jem does not want Scout to walk in the snow or eat it because he considers that a waste of the snow.

10. Miss Maudie's house is on fire and Atticus thinks the children would be safer outside than in the house. He is afraid the fire might spread to their home.

Suggested Essay Topics

1. Describe Miss Maudie's reactions to her home burning. Tell why she was able to behave in this way.

2. Describe the colors of the snowman/woman. Tell how the colors relate to Maycomb. Describe the outward appearance of the snow person and how it changes. Describe the interior of the snow person. Is there symbolism relating to gender bias here? Why, or why not?

Chapter 9

New Characters:

Tom Robinson: *the accused rapist whom Atticus must defend*

Ike Finch: *Maycomb County's sole surviving Confederate veteran*

Aunt Alexandra and Uncle Jimmy Hancock: *Atticus' sister and her husband*

Mr. and Mrs. Henry Hancock and Francis Hancock: *Aunt Alexandra's son, his wife, and their son*

Summary

Cecil Jacobs and others complicate Scout's school life further when they say "Scout Finch's daddy defended niggers." When Scout asks Atticus about this, he says that he does. Atticus explains that he could not hold his head up again if he doesn't defend Robinson, but he does not expect to win the case.

Atticus' family meets Uncle Jack at Aunt Alexandra's for Christmas. Francis, a first cousin-once-removed, tells Scout that Aunt Alexandra says Atticus "let's you all run wild" and "now he's turned into a nigger-lover…" Scout splits her knuckle on his teeth and Jack spanks her for fighting. Later, Scout talks to Uncle Jack about his unfairness in spanking her.

That night Scout eavesdrops on the two brothers. She hears Uncle Jack say half in jest that he is afraid to get married for fear he will have children. The chapter concludes with Atticus discussing the upcoming trial with Uncle Jack.

Analysis

This chapter marks the beginning of a very difficult time for

Scout. It seems as though she faces criticism and conflict every-where she turns. Her classmates criticize Atticus for defending Tom Robinson. Her own cousin Francis also criticizes Atticus and tattles on Scout. Even her Uncle Jack won't listen to her and spanks her.

Throughout all of these confrontations, Scout must struggle with her temper and try to obey Atticus' instructions to use her head instead of her fists. The result of her eventual loss of control is a spanking from her Uncle Jack. And even this proves a more frustrating experience as he won't listen to her excuses for her actions. As the events in Scout's life become increasingly strange and unpleasant, she feels as if she has no one to turn to for her comfort.

The cause of all the misery in Scout's life is the fact that Atticus agreed to defend Tom Robinson. This action is outside of the un-written Maycomb social code. Atticus, perfectly aware of this code, realizes this, but he agrees to defend Tom anyway. He values a more fundamental set of human rights. He is aware that his actions will have unpleasant reactions from the community which will cause problems for his family, but he must remain true to what he feels is right.

Another instance of the social code appearing in this chapter occurs when Uncle Jack and Aunt Alexandra try to teach Scout how to be a young lady. They are trying to teach her the unwritten code so that as she matures, she will accept her proper role in society. In the face of the injustice being done to Tom, these concerns seem trivial.

Many different kinds of education are explored in Chapter 9, and most of them cause problems for Scout. She is uncomfortable with the social education her aunt and uncle try to give her, and her school education does not suit her much better. She feels that she is learning useless things. From her classmates she is learning worse than useless things. She tells Atticus she learned the word "nigger" and he forbids her to use it. Scout also provides an educa-tion for another character in this chapter. She, Jem and Atticus teach her bachelor Uncle Jack about children and families and the complicated ways that they operate.

In this chapter Scout is finding that one can still be brave and yet fight one's battles with the head—not the fists. Her bravery in fighting her own battles contrasts with the cowardice of Francis who, though older, gets his grandmother to fight his battles for him. Another type of bravery is demonstrated by Atticus when he resolves to follow through on a case he knows he cannot win.

Social realism is a dominant theme in Chapter 9. A family reunion with the less-than-ideal family members and ugly displays of prejudice at home and at school are some of the realistic scenes in Chapter 9.

Study Questions

1. Atticus is to defend a member of Calpurnia's church. What is this person's name?

2. What does Scout mean when she says "I was worrying another bone"?

3. Why does Atticus take a case which is causing so much dissension in the neighborhood?

4. How does Aunt Alexandra make Scout unhappy at meal time?

5. Who is Rose Aylmer?

6. Proponents of behavior modification believe that a way to reduce an undesired behavior is to ignore it. Can you think of an undesired behavior in Scout that Atticus sought to extinguish through ignoring it?

7. What is "Maycomb's usual disease" that Atticus hopes that Scout and Jem will not contract?

8. Why does Jack say that he will never marry?

9. Compare and contrast the Christmas gifts that Jem receives and the gifts that Francis receives.

10. How does Jack punish Scout for fighting with Francis?

Answers

1. Tom Robinson is the member of Calpurnia's church whom Atticus has agreed to defend.

2. Scout is concerned with something else.

3. He is asked to take the case, but more importantly, he would be ashamed not to do so. He has respect for himself and others.

4. Aunt Alexandra makes Scout unhappy by making her eat at the small table instead of at the big table with Jem and the adults.

5. Uncle Jack's cat has the name Rose Aylmer.

6. Atticus tries to eliminate Scout's "cussing" by ignoring it. In fact he tells Jack not to pay any attention to her either.

7. Maycomb's usual disease is prejudice.

8. He plans never to marry so he will never have children. Scout has been a trial to him over the holidays.

9. Jem receives a chemistry set and an air rifle. Both are things to play with. Francis receives clothes. He also receives one thing to "play with"—a red book bag to carry his school work in. Francis's gifts are more practical than Jem's.

10. Jack spanks Scout.

Suggested Essay Topics

1. Compare and contrast Atticus and Jack. Consider their methods of disciplining Scout. How are they the same? How are they different? Which person do you think is more effective in getting the desired result? Why do you believe this is true?

2. Describe the outward pressures on Scout to "become a lady." Do you think Atticus applies the same pressures? Why, or why not? Why do you think Atticus behaves in this way?

Chapter 10

New Characters:

Mr. Heck Tate: *the sheriff of Maycomb County*

Tim Johnson: *Mr. Harry Johnson's liver-colored bird dog*

Zeebo: *Calpurnia's son who drives a garbage truck for Maycomb County*

Summary

Jem and Scout feel dissatisfied with their father. Because he is nearly 50 and wears glasses, they see him as feeble. They doubt his manliness. They worry that he has no exciting occupation and does not teach them to shoot their air rifles. It is in a discussion with their father about their rifles that the theme for the whole book—

the mockingbird—begins to emerge. Atticus tells the children that it is a sin to kill a mockingbird. Scout reflects that it is the only time that she ever hears Atticus say it is a sin to do something. He explains that mockingbirds make music. They do not eat up gardens or nest in corncribs. They merely sing for others to enjoy.

Miss Maudie tries to dispel the myth that Atticus is old because she is close to him in age. Even after Miss Maudie explains that Atticus can draw up an air-tight will, play a Jew's Harp, and beat others at checkers, Scout still wishes he "was a devil from hell."

When Calpurnia sees the rabid dog and calls both the sheriff and Atticus, it is Atticus who makes the fatal shot. Scout and Jem find out that Atticus was known as "One-Shot Finch." Their respect for him is increased tremendously.

The episode concludes with Jem calling out that "Atticus is a gentleman, just like me!"

Analysis

Scout believes that the family position in Maycomb could be raised if Atticus would only distinguish himself. She is beginning to seek the approval of society for herself and for Atticus. Her family is not getting as much recognition as she wishes. Perhaps all of the societal criticism of Atticus is beginning to have an effect on Scout and Jem. When Atticus kills the rabid dog, the children are surprised to learn that their father possesses the qualities they thought he lacked. Scout longs to tell others about his skills, but Jem forbids her to. It is a sign of his maturity that he understands why Atticus does not want to flaunt his talents, and why he is not particularly proud of them. Jem is beginning to recognize the quiet qualities which actually make Atticus a good man.

In Chapter 10 Harper Lee makes the reader aware that Atticus is a man to be reckoned with. The image of Atticus that Scout projects up to this point is a child's view; the *characterization* in Chapter 10 shows Atticus in action and Scout develops a new attitude toward her father. Both the reader and Scout now see that Atticus is far from weak and incapable of defending himself and his family. He is peace-loving because "he's civilized in his heart."

Harper Lee uses the element of *surprise* in Chapter 10. The reader is told of Scout and Jem's hunting trip to find birds; one expects them to find a mockingbird and deal with the choice of killing it, but instead they find the rabid dog. Lee also makes the reader experience *suspense* as the dog appears and as the sheriff and Atticus wait on the deserted street for him to walk toward them. The feeling evoked in the reader is *expectancy*, not unlike that the viewer of a western movie feels when the showdown on the main street of town is imminent. Lee employs *symbolism* when Atticus tells the children not to kill a mockingbird. The mockingbird is symbolic of Tom Robinson. *Social realism* is an important feature in Chapter 10; the discrimination that Atticus and the children face because of Atticus's agreeing to take the case is believable for a 1930s Southern town.

Several kinds of bravery are evident in Chapter 10. Atticus proves his bravery when he walks to the middle of the street to meet the rabid dog. But there is a more important kind of bravery that he demonstrates in hiding skills that he is not especially proud of. He is brave enought to live as a good and peace-loving man, honest to his values. It would be easy enough for him to flaunt his flashier abilities and be more popular. But he would probably consider this cowardly, and he would probably not value the admiration this would bring him. This is similar to the bravery he displays in defending Tom Robinson despite strong disapproval. The other prominent theme is that of *maturation.* Jem has discovered that if one feels satisfied with onself, then it does not matter what others think. Jem has now reached a higher stage of moral development and maturity than his younger sister who seeks only the approval of her peers.

Study Questions

1. What action of Atticus's makes him unpopular with the community?

2. What is a Jew's Harp?

3. Why does Scout wish her father was "a devil from hell"?

4. Who does Calpurnia warn about the rabid dog?

5. What nickname did Atticus have at one time?

6. Who is Zeebo?

7. What does Atticus break when he went to face the dog?

8. Was it really "a policy of cowardice" that Scout follows when she agrees not to fight anymore about Atticus?

9. Why is Calpurnia supposed to go to the back door at the Radley Place?

10. Why is Miss Maudie upset when Scout talks about Atticus being old?

Answers

1. Defending Tom Robinson against the accusation of rape is unpopular with the community.

2. A Jew's Harp is a musical instrument played inside the mouth, against the teeth.

3. Scout wants her father to be a devil from hell so she can brag about him to others.

4. Calpurnia warns the Radleys about the rapid dog.

5. He was called One-Shot Finch or Ol' One-Shot.

6. Zeebo is the driver of the garbage trucks.

7. Atticus breaks his glasses.

8. It is not a cowardly act, as it takes more strength to obey her resolution than to give in to anger.

9. At the time there were social rules that people usually followed. A visitor who was "beneath" the person being visited would use the back door.

10. Miss Maudie is upset because she and Atticus are about the same age.

Suggested Essay Topics

1. Atticus had many accomplishments. What were some of these? Jem and Scout did not recognize their father's accomplishments, they wanted him to distinguish himself in other ways. When Atticus killed the dog, Jem decided to keep this silent. Why do you think this happened?

2. Contrast marksmanship with playing the piano, according to Miss Maudie. Explain why Atticus refused to hunt.

Chapter 11

Summary

Jem and Scout pass Mrs. Dubose's home on their way to the store. Because Mrs. Dubose makes sly remarks about Atticus, Jem returns to cut all the buds off her camellia bushes. Atticus confronts Jem with the cut flowers and advises Jem to talk with Mrs. Dubose. Atticus does not allow Scout to go with Jem on this visit, but he comforts her with the statement, "It's not time to worry yet." For punishment, Mrs. Dubose requires Jem and Scout to visit her six days a week for a month and read to her for two hours. She admits to Atticus and the children that she is requiring them to stay longer each day and that she is extending the total time by a week.

About a month after their time is completed, Mrs. Dubose dies. Mrs. Dubose was a morphine addict. After her death Atticus explains to the two children that they helped distract her and helped her die free of any drug addiction. Atticus explains to the children that continuing even when you know you're licked is true courage. He says Mrs. Dubose is the bravest person he knows.

Analysis

Throughout the difficult weeks in which Atticus had been subjected to so much criticism from the community, Jem had been very careful to control his temper and to advise Scout to do the same. In Chapter 11, he finally snaps. The initial confrontation occurs when Mrs. Dubose hurls insults at the children. Jem returns to her house in a rage and cuts all of her prize camellia bushes. Atticus forces Jem to face up to his act and to go talk with Mrs. Dubose. She decides upon his punishment. For over a month he must visit her and read to her for two hours, six days a week.

Although Jem does not realize it at first, this pact requires inner strength from both Jem and Mrs. Dubose. Jem must fight with his anger at all of the cruel things that Mrs. Dubose says about the Finch family. It is difficult for him to be polite to her under these circumstances, but following his father's example, he manages to behave himself. Mrs. Dubose faces an even greater trial. She is forcing herself to overcome an addiction to morphine, a process which requires great willpower and bravery.

Because Mrs. Dubose is an old woman and because she is sick, she can speak her mind more loudly and honestly than most members of the community. Her age and infirmity place her slightly outside of the regular social codes. In this way she is free to express her disapproval of Atticus' actions. Many other people feel the way she does, but up until this point only children have been impolite enough to express their feelings. It is difficult for the children to hear this, and they rely on Atticus' strength and wisdom to help them through this difficult time.

The children's interaction with Mrs. Dubose becomes an important part of their education. Although at first she seems only to be cantankerous and antagonizing, through Atticus they learn of her considerable strength of character. They also learn by her example the true meaning of bravery.

Although Chapter 11 is an *episode* complete within itself, the plot of *To Kill a Mockingbird* is largely a *progressive* plot; the reader must complete the book to resolve all the conflicts.

The *imagery* used by the author helps give the experience of reading to Mrs. Dubose a Gothic air. Jem states that the inside of

Mrs. Dubose's is "...all dark and creepy. There's shadows and things on the ceiling...."

Fears and superstitions are once again important in Chapter 11. However, in this case, the fear centers around Mrs. Dubose's home and its inhabitants, not the Radley Place and the Radleys.

Study Questions

1. Why do Jem and Scout hate Mrs. Dubose at first?

2. What does *apoplectic* mean?

3. What is Atticus's advice to Jem when Mrs. Dubose angers him?

4. Atticus has a special way of greeting Mrs. Dubose which pleases her. Describe the greeting.

5. What things does Atticus require Jem to do to make amends for his rage?

6. What does Atticus say is the one thing that "doesn't abide by majority rule"?

7. Why do you think Atticus brings Scout two yellow pencils and Jem a football magazine after their first session with Mrs. Dubose?

8. Why is Mrs. Dubose lengthening the sessions each time?

9. What is Mrs. Dubose battling?

10. What does Mrs. Dubose give Jem before she dies?

Answers

1. They hate Mrs. Dubose at first because she speaks rudely to them and criticizes Atticus and their family.

2. An *apoplectic* person is one who is likely to have a seizure or a hemorrhage.

3. He encourages Jem to take it easy and reminds Jem that Mrs. Dubose is old and ill. He tells Jem to be a gentleman.

4. He always says "Good evening, Mrs. Dubose. You look like a picture this evening." (He does not say a picture of what!)

5. He requires Jem to visit with Mrs. Dubose and to read to her each day and work in her yard as she requests.

6. Atticus says that one's conscience does not abide by majority rule.

7. He probably brings the gifts to thank them for the visit.

8. She is lengthening the time between her medicines.

9. Mrs. Dubose is battling morphine addiction.

10. Mrs. Dubose gives Jem a single white camellia.

Suggested Essay Topics

1. Describe Mrs. Dubose. Describe her home. Does the setting in which Mrs. Dubose lives seem suited to her personality? Explain.

2. According to Atticus, what is real courage? Give examples of real courage you have seen in *To Kill a Mockingbird.*

Chapter 12

New Characters:

Reverend Sykes: *pastor of First Purchase A.M.E. Zion Church*

Lula: *contentious member of First Purchase A.M.E. Zion Church*

Summary

Part Two of *To Kill a Mockingbird* begins with Chapter 12. The focus shifts from the ghosts and superstitions associated with the Radleys to Tom Robinson.

The children's growth and development are evident as time passes. Atticus has to spend time in Montgomery, so the children are left alone with Calpurnia more and more. One Sunday Calpurnia takes the children to church with her. The children find that they are not warmly accepted by all members of the First Purchase African M.E. Zion Church.

The children find similarities—and differences—between the

church they normally attend and the church to which Calpurnia takes them. On the way home, the children get to know Calpurnia better. They begin to regard her as a fine friend and as a real person with a life separate from her life with them.

This chapter has an open ending. The children find Aunt Alexandra sitting in a rocking chair on their porch when they return from church.

Analysis

In Chapter 12 there is a new sense of distance growing between Jem and Scout. Scout tells how Jem has "...acquired an alien set of values and was trying to impose them on me." Scout says that he has "...acquired a maddening air of wisdom" and "several times he has even told me what to do."

In this chapter, the children once again see evidence of the trouble which can ensue when someone tries to see the world outside of their social circle, or to defy the social codes which fit everyone neatly into an immovable place. They attend church with Calpurnia, and they are surprised at the resistance they meet. They are accosted by a woman named Lula. She questions, "I wants to know why you bringin' white chilluns to nigger church." The children find themselves in conflict with others. They are in a different segment of society. They, not Calpurnia or Tom Robinson, are the outsiders this time. They feel the sting of being "out of their place in society." Jem asks to go home because "they don't want us here." Scout agrees. "I sensed, rather than saw, that we were being advanced upon."

During the sermon Scout hears something which once again makes her feel as if she doesn't quite fit into her supposed place in society. Scout describes the image of the female presented in the sermon that day as the "Impurity of Women Doctrine." The pastor explains that "Bootleggers cause enough trouble in the Quarters, but women were worse." Scout believes this view seems to preoccupy all clergymen. Scout must find this image of women as confusing, when all around her are voices trying to teach her to accept her role as a woman. It is difficult for her to resist the urge of society to conform when even Jem tells her, "It's time you started bein' a girl and acting right." The reader finds that Scout may be weakening when she says, "I began to think there was some skill involved in being a girl."

Sometimes a character's separation from society is not as self-imposed as Scouts and has more deleterious effects. Helen Robinson has been feeling chastised by the community because of the accusations levelled against her husband. "Helen's finding it hard to get work these days…" The reason for her inability to find work is "because of what folks say Tom's done…Folks aren't anxious to—to have anything to do with any of his family."

Dialect is only one of the stylistic devices employed by Lee in *To Kill a Mockingbird* and particularly in Chapter 12. In this chapter the children discover that Calpurnia leads a double life and uses two languages. When Scout asks her "why do you talk nigger-talk…," Cal explains that those in her church would think she was "putting on airs to beat Moses" if she spoke in her church as she did in the children's home. She further explains that she must change who she is to keep from aggravating them. Sometimes "there's nothing you can do but keep your mouth shut or talk their language."

Irony is evident when the children—who have been unaccepted at times in their social groups because their father is defending Tom

Robinson—are unaccepted in the very church that Tom attends. Lee uses *metaphor* (calling something by another name) on page 116:

> ...summer was Dill by the fishpool smoking string, Dill's eyes alive with complicated plans to make Boo Radley emerge; summer was the swiftness with which Dill would reach up and kiss me when Jem was not looking, the longings we sometimes felt each other feel. With him, life was routine; without him, life was unbearable.

The children's education is continued in Chapter 12. This time, however, it is Calpurnia—not Atticus or a school teacher—who instructs Jem and Scout. She takes them to her church, tells them about herself and her education, and advises them on how to get along with others.

Chapter 12 reminds the reader that *To Kill a Mockingbird* is a *novel of maturation (Bildungsroman)*. The lessons the children learn in this chapter help them to grow and mature. Calpurnia begins to call Jem, "Mister Jem." She tells Scout that "...Mister Jem's growing up. He's gonna want to be off to himself a lot now, doin' whatever boys do..."

Prejudice is a dominant theme in Part Two of *To Kill a Mockingbird*. In this chapter the children face discrimination at the First Purchase A.M.E. Zion Church. They also note the different feelings about Atticus—for instance in the Montgomery paper and in the very church in which Tom Robinson is a member. Helen Robinson also feels the sharp edge of discrimination.

Study Questions

1. What change does Calpurnia make in the way she addresses 12-year-old Jem?

2. What does Calpurnia permit Scout to do that she had not permitted before?

3. What does the political cartoon of Atticus chained to a desk and wearing short pants mean to Jem?

4. Why should one not tell all one knows—according to Calpurnia?

5. Why are hymnals not used in the First Purchase A.M.E. Zion Church?

6. How is Zeebo related to Calpurnia?

7. Scout says she is confronted with the Impurity of Women doctrine in the First Purchase Church. What is the doctrine?

8. How does Calpurnia say that people can be changed?

9. Calpurnia says that "Colored folks don't show their ages so fast." What does Jem decide is the reason for this?

10. How is Tom's wife Helen treated after Tom's accusation?

Answers

1. Calpurnia begins to call him "Mister Jem."

2. Calpurnia allows Scout to come into the kitchen to visit.

3. Jem explained that it means that Atticus spends his time doing things that other people would not want to.

4. Calpurnia says one should not tell all one knows, firstly because it is not ladylike and secondly because folks don't like to be around those who know more than they do.

5. Hymnals are not used in the First Purchase A.M.E. Zion Church primarily because most members cannot read.

6. Zeebo, the driver of the garbage truck, is Calpurnia's son.

7. This doctrine, according to Scout, says that women are worse than men.

8. Calpurnia says that folks are not going to change because she is "talkin' right, they've got to want to learn themselves, and when they don't want to learn there's nothing you can do but keep your mouth shut or talk their language."

9. Jem says "colored folks" age less quickly because they do not read.

10. Tom's wife is shunned by white society after the accusation. She cannot find work.

Suggested Essay Topics

1. Describe the double life that Calpurnia leads. Why does she lead this double life?

2. Compare and contrast the church service in Calpurnia's church with a church service in Jem and Scout's church. Why do the differences occur? Do you think the church services in the two churches will become more alike or more different as time goes by? Why?

Chapter 13

Summary

Aunt Alexandra moves in with Scout, Jem, and Atticus "for a while" in order to give Scout some "feminine influence." When Atticus returns from Montgomery he explains to the children why his sister is staying. Scout narrates, however, that Aunt Alexandra's presence is "not so much Atticus' doing as hers."

Maycomb welcomes Aunt Alexandra. She becomes a resident expert on the people of Maycomb and their ancestors, and she tries to instill in the children an appreciation for their own ancestors. Scout remarks that they have already heard of one of these: Cousin Joshua "who went round the bend."

After hearing Scout's opinion, Aunt Alexandra tries to enlist the help of Atticus in teaching the children to value their heritage. Atticus attempts to tell them of their ancestry, but he concludes by saying, "I don't want you to remember it." As he leaves the room, he says, "Get more like Cousin Joshua every day, don't I?"

Analysis

In Chapter 13, we see Atticus trying to teach his children their place in society, but we also see that he is very uncomfortable with this task. Atticus tries to obey Alexandra and tell the children about the family, but he feels uncomfortable "bragging" about something over which he has no control. Scout is just as uncomfortable trying to follow Alexandra's instructions for realizing her place in society. But she follows Atticus' example and tries to control her temper.

In Chapter 13, Harper Lee continues to employ stylistic devices in her writing. *Repetition* is used to drive home a point. It is significant that both Atticus and Jem use one phrase several times in *To Kill a Mockingbird*. Both make use of the line, "It's not time to worry." We hear Jem using that line at the fire on two occasions and Atticus using that line as he discusses the trial with the children, as Scout asks him about Jem and Mrs. Dubose, and during the day that the rabid dog came to their street. The line used by Atticus tends to dispel any sense of foreboding on the part of Scout and the reader. Most readers trust Atticus because they have seen him at work when the rabid dog was in the neighborhood and when he tries to rush the sheriff into action. Like the children, the reader now believes Atticus will let the children (and the reader) know when it is time to worry.

The writer uses an element of *surprise* when she allows Atticus to take back his words in support of the family "heritage" at the end of Chapter 13. "I don't want you to remember it. Forget it." Atticus reappears in the doorway and adds humor to the otherwise tense situation. His raised eyebrows and slipped glasses add humor to his remarks, "Get more like Cousin Joshua [who was locked up] every day, don't I? Do you think I'll end up costing the family five hundred dollars?" Scout, too, adds *humor* to the chapter when Alexandra begins to explore seriously the family tree. Scout asks Aunt Alexandra if the "beautiful character" is the family member who was locked up so long when he "went round the bend at the University."

In this chapter we see two examples of Atticus' rejection of the standard social codes. First of all we see it in his lessons to his children. At first he attempts to teach them their accepted role in society, according to his sister's wishes. But he is uncomfortable with this, and he returns to his initial style of teaching by example, showing his children through his own actions the importance of being true to one's values. In his own life, this belief leads to his second kind of bravery. He prepares to defend Tom Robinson despite the opposition of most of Maycomb and despite the fact that he feels certain of the jury's verdict.

Study Questions

1. Why does Alexandra come to live with the Finch family?

2. What does the word *amanuensis* mean?

3. How does Maycomb receive Alexandra?

4. What does it mean when Scout says that Cousin Joshua "went round the bend"?

5. What is Atticus' remedy for stomach problems?

6. What is Maycomb's primary reason for being?

7. Why does Maycomb always remain about the same size?

8. What message does Alexandra ask Atticus to bring to the children?

9. What does Scout mean when she says that Alexandra has a preoccupation with heredity?

10. What does Scout mean when she says that Alexandra thinks that everybody in Maycomb had a streak?

Answers

1. Alexandra stays with the Finch family in order to give a feminine influence to Scout.

2. The word *amanuensis* means stenographer.

3. Maycomb welcomes Alexandra and includes her in its social life.

4. Scout means that Cousin Joshua had a nervous breakdown.

5. He takes some soda.

6. Government is Maycomb's primary reason for being.

7. It grows inward. Because new people settled there so rarely the families intermarry.

8. Atticus asks the children to live up to their name, as per Alexandra's instructions. She asks that they try to behave like a little lady and a little gentleman.

9. Scout cannot understand why Alexandra is so concerned with a person's ancestry.

10. According to Alexandra, every family in town has some kind of habit such as drinking, fighting, or gambling.

Suggested Essay Topics

1. Compare and contrast Scout's and Alexandra's definitions of "a fine person."

2. Both Jem and Atticus tell Scout that it is not time to worry. What does this tell you about the speakers?

Chapter 14

Summary

The previously serene Finch household is thrown into disarray. The townspeople oppose Atticus' defending Tom Robinson and are making comments. When Scout hears the word "rape" and asks Atticus what it means, he gives a legal definition. This delicate situ-

ation is followed by Scout's request to visit Calpurnia—which Aunt Alexandra immediately vetoes. When Scout tells Aunt Alexandra that she had not been asked, Atticus chastises Scout.

Jem motions for Scout to follow him upstairs where he explains to her that Atticus and Aunt Alexandra have "been fussing." Scout realizes she has never heard anyone quarrel with Atticus. Jem asks Scout not to antagonize Aunt Alexandra since Atticus has "got a lot on his mind now, without us worrying him." Jem tells Scout if she antagonizes their aunt, he will spant her. Scout curses Jem and a fight ensues which brings Atticus to separate them. Aunt Alexandra mutters "…just one of the things I've been telling you about."

The remark from Aunt Alexandra reunites the two children. When Scout walks to her bed she steps on something which she believes is a snake. When Jem brings a broom they find that Dill has run away from home and is hiding under her bed. The children get him a pan of cornbread and once he's satisfied his hunger he weaves stories about how he came to Maycomb from Meridian. The children convince him to tell Atticus that he has run away. When Miss Rachel is told of Dill's adventures, she raises cries of concern. Atticus sums up the night as going "from rape to riot to runaways."

That night Dill climbs into bed with Scout. He explains to her why he ran away and how he actually got to the town of Maycomb. Their conversation concludes with speculations as to why Boo has never run away from home. They decide that he had no place to go.

Analysis

The tension that the Finch family faces because of the Robinson trial is beginning to wear on their nerves and cause conflicts between them. One example is that Scout and Jem feel pitted against each other at times. Another example is that Dill competes with a new father-figure to win the attention of his mother. When Alexandra tries to tell Atticus to fire Calpurnia, once again we see character-against-character conflict. The children unite themselves against Alexandra when they overhear her remark to Atticus that their scuffling is "just one of the things I've been telling you about."

In this chapter we see more evidence of Jem struggling to become an adult. At one moment he is trying to behave as a responsible adult and cautioning Scout not to worry Atticus. A few minutes later he is fighting with Scout and Atticus has to come to separate the two. A little later Jem is behaving as a responsible adult by bringing Atticus into the room to show him that Dill is there.

Many of the people in Maycomb are opposed to Atticus's representing Tom Robinson. Atticus is determined to do what he himself thinks is right despite their opposition. He sets himself against Maycomb society. In the face of the serious problems, Alexandra continues to worry about more trivial ones and pushes for Scout to assume a more lady-like role and to remember her breeding. Dill's parents, too, expect him to behave like a boy and not be underfoot all the time. Scout, Atticus, and Dill all fail to live up to the expectations of society.

In Chapter 14 the reader continues to see the emergence of the *maturational novel,* especially through the character of Jem. Scout and Dill, however, continue to possess an air of innocence—which is especially evident when the two lie in bed and discuss where babies come from.

Study Questions

1. What does Scout find under her bed?

2. What does Atticus mean when he says, "…rape to riot to runaways"?

3. Why does Dill run away?

4. What does Scout think is under her bed at first?

5. What is Scout's response to Aunt Alexandra when she tells Scout that she cannot visit Calpurnia?

6. What does Scout mean by "…he bore with fortitude her Wait Till I Get You Home…"

7. When Scout asked Atticus if she could go to Calpurnia's, what was Alexandra's reaction?

8. Whom does Atticus tell Scout to mind?

9. Why does Scout seem to be a very innocent child?

10. Why does Jem ask Scout not to antagonize Aunt Alexandra?

Answers

1. Scout finds Dill under her bed.

2. In one night Atticus had dealt with Scout's questions about the word *rape*, had broken up a fight between Scout and Jem, and had dealt with the runaway Dill.

3. Dill says that he believes his parents get along better without him. He says that they expect him to behave like a boy.

4. Scout thinks at first that a snake is under her bed.

5. Scout says that she did not ask Aunt Alexandra.

6. This is a reference to the various "speeches" Dill's Aunt Rachel gives when she finds Dill has run away.

7. Alexandra immediately says that Scout cannot go.

8. Atticus says Scout has to mind Calpurnia, Alexandra, and him.

9. Scout seems to be especially innocent when she and Dill lie in bed discussing where babies come from. She also seems innocent because she does not know the word *rape*.

10. Jem does not want Scout to antagonize Alexandra because Atticus has a lot on his mind thinking of the upcoming trial.

Suggested Essay Topics

1. Compare Dill's fictional and factual accounts of running away.

2. What evidence do you see that Jem is growing up? What evidence do you see that Jem is not yet an adult?

Chapter 15

New Characters:

Braxton Bragg Underwood: *sole owner, editor, and printer of* The
    Maycomb Tribune

Mr. Walter Cunningham: *the father of Walter Cunningham and a
    member of the mob which appears at the jail*

Dr. Reynolds: *the family doctor of the Finch family and most of the
    people in Maycomb*

Summary

After numerous calls, much pleading, and a letter, Dill finally
receives permission to remain in Maycomb. Scout says that they
only had "a week of peace together…A nightmare was upon us."

A group of men from Maycomb visit Atticus at home on Saturday night to tell him that they are uneasy about Tom in the jail.
They question Atticus' motives for taking the case. Atticus tells them
that he will continue to help Tom and will see that the truth is told
in court. At this point the crowd approaches Atticus. Jem breaks
the tension by telling him that the phone is ringing.

After a quiet Sunday afternoon, Atticus leaves the house. The
three children follow him and find him at the jail, sitting outside
with a long extension cord and a light at the end. A mob gathers
at the jail just after the children arrive. As the men in the mob
move menacingly forward, the children make the presence
known. Atticus orders the children to leave, but they refuse. One
of the men threatens Jem, and they give Atticus 15 seconds to get
the kids out.

Scout defuses a tense situation by talking directly to Mr. Walter
Cunningham—a member of the mob—and reminding him of his
ties to the Finch family. She reminds him that his son Walter is her
classmate. Mr. Cunningham orders the mob to get going.

After the mob leaves, the Finches and Dill find that Underwood
had them covered with his shotgun the whole time. Dill carries
Atticus' chair as they all walk home together.

Analysis

In this chapter we see what a dangerous position Atticus has put himself in by defying certain social codes. This is especially evident during a confrontation in front of the jail. The mob which opposes Tom for his supposed "crime" and his color demands that Atticus move out of the way so that they can enter the jail. Atticus refuses to stir. A less violent example of character-against-society conflict occurs when the children want to look out the window at the company. Alexandra cautions Jem not to "disgrace the family." She also expresses her concern with "Southern womanhood." Atticus, however, relegates it all to its proper perspective when he

says he is, "in favor of Southern womanhood as much as anybody, but not for preserving polite fiction at the expense of human life."

In Chapter 15 we see how people who constitute a mob often act very differently than they would alone—even to the point of defying their morals. Individual members of the mob must have felt pulled in varying directions. Walter Cunningham clearly faces a conflict of interests in the chapter. He is a member of the mob, but he is faced with his individuality when Scout singles him out and talks with him. He becomes a leader—not just a member—of the mob. He orders the men to leave and chooses right even though he is in the minority.

Repetition is an important device in Chapter 15. Scout tells the reader about Atticus' "dangerous question" which always precedes action on Atticus' part. The action may be jumping an opponent's game pieces in checkers or winning an argument. The question is "Do you really think so?" Each time the reader sees it, they know that something is going to happen. Atticus asks the question twice in the chapter.

In this chapter we see the bravery of children pitted against the cowardliness of mob members. Scout and Jem turn out to be the real heroes when they break the tension on two occasions. When the men begin to move ominously toward Atticus, Jem deliberately breaks the tension by telling Atticus that the phone is ringing. Scout breaks the tension when she singles out a member of the mob and talks with him about his child. Scout shows her bravery when she physically attacks the man who grabs Jem by the collar. Atticus is determined to protect the man he is defending even in the face of a mob; this is bravery. Mr. Cunningham's bravery is evident when he steps out from the mob and tells the group to go home.

Study Questions

1. What are the only two reasons grown men stand outside in the yard, according to Scout?

2. What is meant by a "change of venue?"

3. Who is the mockingbird in this chapter? Why?

4. Who does Scout recognize in the mob at the jail?

5. Contrast the way Atticus rises from his chair at the jail and the way that he normally rises from a chair.

6. What breaks the tension when the mob comes to the house?

7. Where is Tom during the time that Atticus faces the mob downtown?

8. What does Calpurnia mean when she says Jem has the "look-arounds?"

9. What attitude do most of the people in Maycomb have toward walking?

10. What is Atticus's loaded question?

Answers

1. Grown men stand outside for death and politics.

2. A change of venue is a change in the place where the jury is selected and the trial is held or where the events occur.

3. Tom is the mockingbird. Atticus could also be considered a mockingbird since he is endangered and he has done nothing to harm anyone. Since the reader is developing sympathy for Arthur, he might be a mockingbird also.

4. Scout recognizes Mr. Cunningham.

5. Atticus normally rises from a chair very quickly, but at the jail he moves like an old man.

6. Jem shouts that the phone is ringing in order to break the tension.

7. Tom is in the Maycomb jail.

8. It means that he is curious.

9. People only walk if they have a place to go.

10. Atticus' loaded question is "Do you really think so?"

Suggested Essay Topics

1. Compare and contrast the events of the Saturday night and the events of Sunday evening.

2. Discuss the bravery of the children, especially in contrast to the cowardly mob.

Chapter 16

New Characters:

Judge Taylor: *presides over the session of court in which Tom Robinson is to be tried*

Mr. Dolphus Raymond: *a white man who sits with the black people and who has "a colored woman and all sorts of mixed chillun."*

Foot-washers: *a man and his wife who belong to a church which is conservative and practices the washing of feet*

Idlers' Club: *old men who spend their last days idling on benches on the town square and who serve as courthouse critics*

Summary

Jem, Scout, and Atticus come home on Sunday night after Aunt Alexandra is in bed. They coast into the carhouse and enter the house without a word. As Scout begins to drift into sleep, she sees

Atticus standing in the middle of an empty street pushing up his glasses. She begins crying, but Jem does not tease her about it.

The next morning appetites are very delicate. Alexandra complains that the children were out late the night before, but Atticus says that he is glad that they had come along. When Aunt Alexandra says that Mr. Underwood was there all the time, Atticus says that it was strange that Underwood was there since "He despises Negroes, won't have one near him." Alexandra chastises Atticus for talking "like that in front of them." Atticus responds that Calpurnia knows how important she is to the family and that he is sure she knows about Mr. Underwood also.

Atticus talks about the fact that the mob is really made of people. He praises Scout's actions and suggests that the police force should be made up of children.

Jem, Dill, and Scout stand in their yard after breakfast and watch the steady parade of people going to the trial. Jem calls their names and tells a bit about each to Dill. None of these characters actually speak except the foot-washers, who hurl Bible verses at Miss Maudie. She throws a verse back in their direction.

Miss Maudie is working in her yard, but Miss Stephanie says she is going to the courthouse. Miss Maudie smilingly cautions Miss Stephanie to be careful that she does not get a subpoena since she knows so much about the case.

Jem explains to the other two about Mr. Dolphus Raymond's habit of drinking whiskey and about his "colored woman and all sorts of mixed chillun." Jem advises the others that "around here once you have a drop of Negro blood, that makes you all black."

That afternoon the three slip away to the courthouse. Scout hears the Idlers' Club of old men sitting on benches in the square talking about Atticus. Scout finds out that the court appointed Atticus to defend Tom Robinson.

When the children find that there are no seats available downstairs in the courthouse, Reverend Sykes invites them upstairs. The children are able to see everything well from the balcony. Judge Taylor, they find, permits smoking in his courtroom and he munches on a dry cigar himself. When the children get to their seats, the first witness is already on the stand. Mr. Heck Tate is speaking.

Analysis

In Chapter 16, all of the tension that was mounting seems to burst, as the day of the trial finally arrives. This is apparent even between or among the characters. Atticus has tried to be patient and understanding with his sister, but in this chapter he almost gives in to anger. He restrains himself, however, and Scout notices his feelings only as a subtle change in his behavior towards Alexandra, a "digging in." Scout herself gives in to the fear and confusion she feels and bursts with tears. Jem recognizes her emotions, because although he hears her crying he "is nice about it" and does not make fun of her or remind her that she is too old to cry.

In this chapter we meet several characters who live outside of society because they choose to. Mr. Dolphus Raymond is one. He lives outside of town and he has "a colored woman and all sorts of mixed chillun." This opens him to much criticism and speculation from the community. Miss Maudie, although she functions comfortably in society, is not afraid to speak her mind when someone tries to criticize her. When the foot-washing Baptists openly harangue her as they drive by her house, she is quick to respond with their own ammunition—quoting pertinent Biblical passages to them.

A more tragic example of people who are outside of society through no power or choice of their own are the children of black and white parents. Jem describes how they don't quite fit any place in society. They are treated worse than even those who occupy the lowest positions in the social structure. They are ignored and neglected.

Jem and Scout find themselves out of their usual social position in this chapter, but comfortably so. When there is no room for them to sit downstairs in the courtroom, they are welcomed into the balcony where the black people sit. Both literally and metaphorically this gives them a new perspective on the trial.

In Chapter 16 Harper Lee continues to employ stylistic devices in her writing. *Repetition* is used when Atticus says that Scout made Mr. Cunningham "walk in his shoes" or skin. Scout uses a *comparison* when she compares Atticus' meeting the mob with Atticus's meeting the rabid dog. Characters in the chapter continue to use 1930s Southern *dialect*. For example, Jem speaks of "Co-Cola."

The classroom for Chapter 16 is the yard as the children watch the people pour into town and the courtroom itself. The theme of *maturation* is evident when Scout asks for coffee, a *symbol* of maturation. Calpurnia says at first Scout is too little, but she relents and gives her coffee mixed with milk, a symbol of increased maturity.

Study Questions

1. Who presides over Tom's trial?

2. What does the word *elucidate* mean?

3. What makes one a Mennonite, according to Jem?

4. What does Atticus say is the result of naming people after Confederate generals?

5. What does Atticus say had brought the mob to its senses?

6. What is the Idlers' Club?

7. With whom do the children sit in court?

8. What two things keep Mr. Raymond from being trash?

9. What do the foot-washers say to Miss Maudie?

10. Why does Aunt Alexandra criticize Atticus?

Answers

1. Judge Taylor presides over Tom Robinson's trial.

2. *Elucidate* means to explain or to clarify.

3. Mennonites don't use buttons, they live deep in the woods, trade across the river, rarely come to Maycomb, and have blue eyes. The men do not shave after they marry.

4. Atticus says the naming made them steady drinkers.

5. Atticus says an eight-year-old brought the mob to its senses.

6. The Idlers' Club is a group of retired men who frequent the court and the courthouse.

7. The children sit with Reverend Sykes.

8. Mr. Raymond is from an old family and owns land.

9. The foot-washers yell "He that cometh in vanity departeth in darkness."

10. Aunt Alexandra criticizes Atticus for talking about Mr. Underwood's racist feelings in front of Calpurnia.

Suggested Essay Topics

1. Describe Judge Taylor. What do you think was unusual about him? What kind of courtroom did he run?

2. Describe the day of the trial in Maycomb. Is there another event in a small town to which the event could be likened? Why do you think so many people attended?

Chapter 17

New Characters:

Mr. Gilmer: *the solicitor*

Robert E. Lee Ewell: *the father of the victim of Tom's alleged rape*

Summary

Chapter 17 is a record of the court proceedings as told from Scout's point of view. The reader hears Mr. Tate tell about the day he was called to see Mayella. Mr. Ewell, the father of the victim allegedly raped by Tom, is also cross-examined. He testifies that he saw Tom raping Mayella.

Reverend Sykes wants to send Scout home when Ewell describes certain explicit parts of the alleged rape, but Jem assures him that she does not understand.

The chapter concludes with Robert Ewell's testimony during which it is proved that he is left-handed. Scout comments that this shows that Ewell himself could have beaten Mayella and caused the bruises on the right side of her face, but she cautions Jem and the reader not to count their chickens before they are hatched.

Analysis

This chapter is very tense as witnesses are questioned. The reader senses the conflict and knows a life is at stake. At one point Atticus argues with Mr. Gilmer. The tension increases when Mr. Ewell testifies. He seems to be careful as he speaks so that he will not be caught in a lie. He seems to have trouble understanding Atticus' questions at many points. One wonders if he might be wrestling with his conscience, but such a struggle does not openly reveal itself.

Atticus is defending Tom against the white society in Maycomb. Like many Southern towns they seem to hold white women on a pedestal. When the white "victim" says that Tom has beaten and raped her, he is pitted against the society which seems to take any white woman's word over that of any black person.

To Kill a Mockingbird continues to be a *maturational novel.* When the testimony becomes explicit, Judge Taylor receives a request that women be cleared from the courtroom, but he decides to delay. The Reverend Sykes is concerned that Scout should leave also, because she might understand. Scout is still innocent, but she tries to appear more mature than she is. She tells the Reverend she does indeed understand, but Jem is able to convince the Reverend that she does not; both the children are, therefore, able to stay.

In Chapter 17 Harper Lee continues to employ stylistic devices in her writing. She uses a *malapropism* to create *humor* and relieve tension during the courtroom drama. For instance, when Mr. Ewell is asked if he is ambidextrous, he says that he can use one hand as well as the other. Lee uses *onomatopoeia* when Scout says the sound of the gavel is "pink-pink-pink." The 1930s Southern *dialect* (everyday speech) is the speech of the people in the courtroom. For example, "was fetched by Bob—by Mr. Bob Ewell Yonder, one night—"

Study Questions

1. What is the name of the solicitor?

2. What does the word *ambidextrous* mean?

3. Why does Reverend Sykes ask Jem to take Dill and Scout home from the trial?

4. Where do the Ewells live?

5. Why does Scout get to stay during the explicit testimonies?

6. Where do Scout and Jem sit during the trial?

7. What does Scout mean when she says that Jem is counting his chickens?

8. Why is it important that Mr. Ewell signs his name with his left hand?

9. What excuse does Jem use for not taking Scout home?

10. What does it mean when Scout says the Ewells live as guests of the county?

Answers

1. The solicitor is Mr. Gilmer.

2. *Ambidextrous* means able to use both hands.

3. Reverend Sykes asks Jem to take Scout home because of the explicit details of the rape given during the trial.

4. They live "behind the town garbage dump in what had been a Negro cabin."

5. Scout stays because Jem tells Reverend Sykes that she does not understand.

6. The children sit in the balcony during the trial.

7. It means Jem was counting on Atticus's winning too soon.

8. It is significant that Mr. Ewell uses his left hand to write his name because it shows that he is left-handed. His daughter had bruises on the right side of her face which meant a left-handed person had hit her.

9. Jem says that Scout did not understand what was being said.

10. Scout means that the Ewells are on public welfare.

Suggested Essay Topics

1. Describe the Ewell home. Compare it and contrast it to the home in which Scout and Jem had grown up in Maycomb.

2. Why did Jem think Tom would be found innocent? Why was Scout more hesitant to believe that way?

Chapter 18

New Character:

Mayella Ewell: *the alleged rape victim*

Summary

Chapter 18 is primarily an account of Mayella Ewell's testimony. When Mr. Gilmer begins his questioning, Mayella does not answer his questions about the alleged rape. She tells the judge that she is frightened by Atticus. As she finally begins to tell her story of what she says happened, she seems to grow in confidence. When Atticus begins his cross-examination, he is patient and calm with Mayella. Mayella admits that her father "does tollable" except when he has been drinking. She contradicts this statement by saying that he has never touched a hair on her head. Mayella says she does not know how Tom did it, but he did take advantage of her. Atticus has Tom stand and asks Mayella to identify him. It is then that the full court can see that Tom has a bad arm.

Atticus concludes his questioning by asking Mayella if Tom or Mr. Ewell was the one who beat her. He asks what Mr. Ewell really saw in the window. Mayella does not answer. Finally Mayella says she has something to add. Her final words are, "That nigger yonder took advantage of me an' if you fine fancy gentlemen don't wanta do nothin' about it then you're all yellow stinkin' cowards, the lot of you."

Atticus says that he has one more witness and the chapter concludes.

Analysis

Mayella's testimony is as tense as her father's was. Mayella seems to see Atticus as her accuser. She claims fear of him in the court.

Mayella tries to testify in a convincing manner. It seems evident to the reader that at times Mayella seems to want to tell the truth, but she struggles to keep to her story. For instance, she admits that her father is "tollable" except when he drinks, but she will not admit that he beats her.

The Ewell family does not really fit into Maycomb society. Mayella is conscious of her lower class background. She feels others are better than she and that they are laughing at her. She is very insecure. Mayella also brings racial conflicts into her testimony. She concludes by saying that "That nigger yonder" raped her and that the jury is a bunch of cowards if they do not find him guilty. She is making the conflict white against blacks, rather than truth against falsehood.

In Chapter 18 Harper Lee depicts faithfully Mayella's Southern *dialect*. For instance, she says, "He does tollable…"

The chapter ends as a *cliffhanger*; the reader must read on to hear Tom's testimony.

Study Questions

1. What is Mayella's full name?
2. What are *lavations*?
3. How can Jem tell which characters do not wash regularly?
4. Why does Judge Taylor not hold Mayella in contempt of court?
5. Why is Tom's left arm crippled?
6. Whom does Mayella say she is afraid of?
7. What is a *chiffarobe*?
8. What question does Atticus ask Mayella that makes her furious?
9. What does the word *tollable* mean?
10. How many witnesses does Atticus say he still has to call when Mayella had finished?

Answers

1. Mayella's full name is Mayella Violet Ewell.
2. *Lavations* are washings.

3. Jem says that those who do not wash regularly have a scalded look as if their bodies have been deprived of a protective layer of dirt.

4. She is poor and ignorant.

5. He has caught his left arm in a cotton gin and has torn the muscles loose from the bones.

6. Mayella says she is afraid of Atticus.

7. A *chiffarobe* is an old dresser full of drawers on one side.

8. Atticus asks Mayella if her father had attacked her.

9. The word should read *tolerable*, which means passable.

10. Atticus says he has one witness to call.

Suggested Essay Topics

1. Is Mayella telling the truth or is she lying? What does she say and do in court that makes you feel this way?

2. Describe Atticus' behavior in court toward Mayella. How do you think he feels about her and what she says?

Chapter 19

New Character:

Link Deas: *the former employer of Tom Robinson*

Summary

Chapter 19 tells of Tom's examination and a part of his cross-examination. During the examination by Atticus, Tom tells how he helped Mayella on several occasions. He tells how Mayella hugged him about the waist on the day in question, how Mr. Ewell appeared on the scene, and how Tom ran in fear.

At that point Link Deas stands up and announces, "I just want the whole lot of you to know one thing right now. That boy's worked for me eight years an' I ain't had a speck o'trouble outa him. Not a speck." The judge tells Deas to shut up and throws him out of court.

Mr. Gilmer cross-examines Tom. During the questioning Tom says that he helped Mayella because he felt sorry for her. Scout believes these words are a mistake. Mr. Gilmer calls Tom "boy" each time he addresses him. Suddenly Dill begins to cry and Scout leaves with him. Outside the courtroom they see Mr. Deas. Dill tries to explain that things do not seem right in the courtroom. Mr. Raymond, who is also waiting outside the courtroom, overhears Dill and approaches to talk with the children.

Analysis

Tom's testimony and cross-examination is difficult on many levels. Mr. Gilmer adopts an air of hostility against Tom to capitalize on the prejudice already felt against him. This hostility is so strong that even Dill, who probably does not understand its source, can sense it. He breaks into tears and must be taken from the courtroom. In the face of this hostility Tom attempts to restrain himself and answer the questions properly.

Clearly, Tom seems pitted against many members of the white society as he attempts to respond from the witness stand. Reference is made also to the fact that Mayella is a part of the society that others in Maycomb frown upon. Tom mentions that he feels sorry for her and Scout also makes reference to the fact that Mayella is a member of the lower class and has few friends.

The *mockingbird theme* is very evident in Chapter 19. Tom has not harmed anyone. Although he was being helpful, he has been treated cruelly.

Examples of Tom Robinson's *dialect* (everyday speech) abound in the courtroom interrogation. "She says she never kissed a grown man before an' she might as well kiss a nigger. She says what her papa do to her don't count." Gilmer's *dialect* is also evident as he calls Tom "boy" and causes Dill to be sick by his treatment of Tom.

Lee makes use of many stylistic devices to tell her story. For example, Scout employs *repetition* when she says what Miss Maudie has said earlier about Atticus: "He's the same in the courtroom as he is on the public streets." Harper Lee uses *irony* subtly when

Mayella and Bob Ewell accuse Tom of lusting after a white woman when the reverse is actually true.

Bravery versus cowardice is evident as Atticus and Tom continue to battle for truth and right even though the conclusion seems to be foregone. There is only one reference to Boo Radley and the *motif of ghosts and superstitions:* a comparison is made between the loneliness of Mayella and that of Arthur. This important theme in Part One has been replaced in Part Two.

Study Questions

1. Why is Dill crying?

2. How old is Tom?

3. What is Link Deas' opinion of Tom?

4. What does Judge Taylor say to Deas when he speaks in favor of Tom?

5. What does Tom say that Mr. Ewell saw through the window?

6. Why does Scout take Dill from the courtroom?

7. What does Scout say is a sure sign of guilt?

8. What does Scout mean when she says Maycomb gives the Ewells "the back of its hand"?

9. Why was Tom afraid to push Mayella out of the way?

10. When Tom was approached by Mayella, he did something which Scout says was a sure sign of guilt. What was it?

Answers

1. Dill is crying because of the way that Gilmer treated Tom.

2. Tom is 25.

3. Link says that Tom had worked for him for eight years and he had not had "a speck o'trouble outa him."

4. The judge throws Deas out of the courtroom.

5. He sees Mayella grab Tom and kiss him. Tom was trying to get away.

6. Scout took Dill from the courtroom because he began to cry.

7. Scout says that running is a sure sign of guilt.

8. Scout means that Maycomb gave the Ewells a slap. They gave the Ewells gifts but not in love.

9. Tom "would not have dared strike a white woman under any circumstances and expect to live long…"

10. Tom ran, which Scout considers a sign of guilt.

Suggested Essay Topics

1. Contrast and compare the style of Atticus' and Gilmer's cross-examinations.

2. Compare and contrast Mayella's and Tom's style of answering questions and compare their testimonies. How are they alike? How are they different?

Chapter 20

Summary

After visiting with Raymond and finding out that he makes himself out "badder'n" he is already, Dill and Scout rush back into the courthouse. They find that Atticus is finishing up his summary. Atticus talks to the jury as if he were talking to an individual, concluding with the statement, "In the name of God, believe him." Just as he finishes, Calpurnia makes her way down the center aisle of the courtroom.

Analysis

In this chapter we see a side of human nature which lies below the social codes that people are taught. No matter what role people play in society, they are probably similar underneath. Perhaps the rules of society were set up initially to hide these feelings. Atticus reminds the entire courtroom of the evil side of human nature which everyone faces: the tendency to lie, to do immoral things, and to look with desire on others.

Atticus tries to appeal to the humanity and morality of the jury when he reminds them to do its duty and return Tom Robinson to his home. The jury has a difficult decision to make. Many are fighting their consciences as they determine to convict Tom.

Society in Maycomb involves a caste/racial bias; this bias is evident in the "assumption—the evil assumption—that *all* Negroes lie..." There is a sex bias in the society of Maycomb; most people in the South put the women on a pedestal. Mayella goes against the expectations of society with her actions. "She did something that in our society is unspeakable: she kissed a black man." Another example of character-against-society occurs when certain persons try to get ahead. Getting ahead is difficult for them; they have to battle society. Others are able to get ahead more easily. "some people have more opportunity because they're born with it..." All types of conflict are evident in Chapter 20.

In Chapter 20 Atticus uses a statement that he used before; this is an example of *repetition*. He tells the court that his pity for Mayella does not "extend so far as to her putting a man's life at stake, which she has done in an effort to get rid of her own guilt...."

The *theme of education* is brought out by Atticus in his summation. He says on page 205 that the

> "most ridiculous example I can think of is that the people who run public education promote the stupid and idle along with the industrious—because all men are created equal, educators will gravely tell you, the children left behind suffer terrible feelings of inferiority."

Mr. Raymond also gives the children a lesson when he says, "Cry about the simple hell people give other people—without even thinking."

Bravery versus cowardice (a secondary theme) is evident in this chapter as Atticus continues to work toward a goal that he knows is unachievable; according to his definition, he himself is the epitome of true bravery.

Study Questions

1. What does Dolphus Raymond give Dill to settle his stomach?

2. What is unusual about Atticus's clothing during his final summation?

3. What does Atticus argue are some of the reasons that Tom should not be convicted?

4. How does Atticus end his summation?

5. What does Atticus do in court that the children never saw him do even at home?

6. What feeling do both Tom and Atticus have for Mayella?

7. What does Atticus say is a great leveler?

8. Why does Mr. Raymond share this secret with the children?

9. Why does Mr. Raymond pretend to drink?

10. Does Atticus say that kissing Tom was a crime?

Answers

1. Mr. Raymond gives Dill Coca-Cola to settle his stomach.

2. Atticus's clothing is unusual during final summation because he removes his coat, unbuttons his vest and collar, and loosens his tie. Scout had never seen him do this before in private or in public.

3. Atticus says the state has not produced any medical evidence that the crime that Tom was charged with ever took place.

4. Atticus ends his summation with the words, "In the name of God, believe him."

5. Atticus removes his coat, unbuttons his vest and collar, and loosens his tie.

6. Atticus pities her; Tom feels sorry for her. These emotions are the same.

7. Atticus says the courts were a great leveler.

8. Raymond says he could share his secret with the children because they would understand.

9. Since people could "never understand that I live like I do because that's the way I want to live," Raymond pretends to drink to give them a reason for his life-style.

10. Atticus describes Mayella's kissing Tom as a violation of a social code but not as a crime.

Suggested Essay Topics

1. Give a summary of Atticus's final speech to the jury. Why do you think that he loosened his clothing and removed his coat before he began?

2. Describe Atticus's view of lies and immorality. Do you think his view is typical of most of Maycomb society? Why, or why not?

3. What was the unwritten social code that Mayella broke? Are there unwritten social codes that Atticus himself has in his life?

Chapter 21

Summary

Calpurnia comes to the courtroom to tell Atticus that the children are missing. The children go home to eat, but Atticus says that they can return to hear the verdict. Late in the night the jury convicts Tom. As Atticus leaves by the center aisle, Scout notices that "All around us and in the balcony on the opposite wall the Negroes were getting to their feet."

Analysis

As the jury breaks to make its decision, the reader and the characters have time to reflect on all that has happened. Many of the themes which have been explored throughout the novel come together here. This is the climax in Atticus' long struggle. Because of certain laws in Maycomb society regarding rape and race, the jury's verdict will undoubtedly be against Tom Robinson. Atticus' action despite the predetermined result helps him to epitomize bravery. We know that the jury is torn as they cast their votes. They have to choose between what they know is right and what society has taught them to believe.

In Chapter 21 the fulfillment of *the mockingbird theme* comes to pass. Tom is convicted—but because of his color and not of his guilt. Atticus, who has struggled hard to help Tom, loses the case. The feelings that Scout has in waiting for the decision remind her of a cold morning when the mockingbirds were not singing, a *foreshadowing* of what is to come.

In Chapter 21 Harper Lee continues to employ stylistic devices in her writing. *Foreshadowing* is employed when Reverent Sykes says, "Now don't you be so confident, Mr. Jem, I ain't ever seen any jury decide in favor of a colored man over a white man." The reader is grateful for this foreshadowing which lessens the blow when the jury declares its verdict. Calpurnia's 1930s Southern *diction* (everyday speech) is expressed. "—skin every one of you alive, the very idea, you children listenin' to all that!"

The characterization is a strong point of *To Kill a Mockingbird*. The reader cares what happens to Atticus, Tom, and even to Mayella. Most classics contain this type of characterization. It is the characters that keep classics alive; the plot alone is never sufficient to make a classic.

Study Questions

1. Who walks down the middle aisle carrying a note to Atticus?

2. Why does Reverend Sykes ask Scout to stand when her father passes?

3. How does Reverend Sykes address Scout?

4. What things are strange about the courtroom during the wait for a jury decision?

5. Scout compares the atmosphere in the courthouse before the jury returns to another time and place. What is the time and place?

6. Why is Reverend Sykes not sure that the jury would decide in favor of Tom Robinson?

7. Why does Reverend Sykes's voice seem distant after the decision even though he is standing next to Scout?

8. What does Calpurnia's note say?

9. Why does Atticus walk down the middle aisle?

10. How can you tell when a jury has convicted a defendent?

Answers

1. Calpurnia walks down the aisle carrying a note to Atticus.

2. The whole balcony stands as a sign of respect to Atticus.

3. The Reverend Sykes addresses Scout as "Miss Jean Louise."

4. The courtroom is very quiet. Occasionally a baby will cry out or a child might leave, but the adults sit or stand as still as if they were in church.

5. Scout likens the waiting to the time the rabid dog was near.

6. He is not confident because he has never seen "a jury decide in favor of a colored man over a white man."

7. His voice seems distant or detached because he wants to separate himself from what had happened. He is thinking of other things now.

8. Calpurnia's note says that the children have been missing since noon.

9. Atticus probably walks down the middle aisle to show he is not ashamed of his actions. This walk is an indication of his bravery.

10. When a jury has convicted a defendant, they will not look at the defendant when they return to the courtroom.

Suggested Essay Topics

1. Describe Atticus' actions after the trial. What was the significance of each action?

2. What impressions did Scout have as she waited for the decision?

Chapter 22

Summary

Jem cries angry tears as Atticus, Scout, Jem, and Dill make their way home. Aunt Alexandra is waiting up for them and she tells Atticus, "I'm sorry Brother." Atticus tells his sister that it is fine that the children experienced the trial because it is as much a part of Maycomb County as her teas. He tells Jem that the thing that happened had happened before and would happen again. Then he asks not to be disturbed the next morning.

On the morning after the trial the Finch family discusses the events of the previous day. Atticus assures the children that there will be an appeal. Calpurnia shows Atticus the chicken that Tom Robinson's father has given to him, and asks the family to go into the kitchen to see the gifts from the community. Atticus wipes his eyes and instructs Calpurnia to tell the friends that times are too hard for them ever to do this again.

The children talk with Miss Maudie later in the morning. Miss Stephanie comes over with her questions and her opinions. Miss Maudie tells her to hush and takes the children inside for cake. She allows Jem to talk about the trial and then gives them some information. She tells them that Judge Taylor named Atticus to defend Tom Robinson for his own reasons. She explained that he could have named Maxwell Green, Maycomb's newest lawyer and one who needed experience.

When the children go outside with Miss Maudie, they see Miss Stephanie and Mr. Avery waving wildly at them. They learn from Miss Stephanie that Bob Ewell has threatened Atticus and has spat in his face.

Analysis

In Chapter 22 we see how miserable someone can be if they don't fit into the role society prepares for them. Dill in unhappy and displeased with himself and his life. He wants to please others and himself but finds it very difficult to do both. He announces that his career plans have changed. He plans to become a clown and laugh at people rather than having them laugh at him. Truman Capote, after whom Dill is modeled, also experienced the laughter of others because he was considered effeminate.

When Miss Stephanie and Mr. Avery gossip about Atticus and criticize the children for sitting in the "colored balcony," we see a different example of people causing trouble by moving beyond their societal boundaries. Although this seating arrangement was harmless and practical for Scout and Jem, it was shocking in the eyes of the community. In the town of Maycomb racism is a pervasive and poisonous social code.

Harper Lee makes use of stylistic devices in Chapter 22. Scout uses *foreshadowing* when she remarks the night of the trial that "things are always better in the morning." Harper Lee uses *repetition* to allow the reader and the children to draw strength from Atticus. He tells Jem and Scout before they go to bed that it is "not time to worry yet." Aunt Alexandra demonstrates *sympathy*, a side of her nature the reader has not seen before. Chapter 22 has a *cliffhanger* ending in the threat on Atticus' life.

The chapter presents many people's reactions to the trial of Tom Robinson. The children, especially, were confused and upset by it. The taunting of Mr. Avery and Miss Stephanie only made it more difficult for them. However when Miss Maudie speaks to them, she tries to teach them a new way to look at the situation. She shows them the subtle ways in which people broke the rules of society in order to help Tom Robinson. She also reinforces once again the strength and bravery of Atticus. Compared to him Miss Stephanie and Mr. Avery seem even more cowardly and superficial.

Although some examples of people operating against the expectations society holds for them result in good behavior, Robert Ewell represents the opposite extreme. He lives, literally and figuratively, outside of the community. He seems to represent basest instincts of humanity and acts as a malevolent force when he threatens Atticus. It becomes clear that he considers himself outside the law as well.

Study Questions

1. What does Aunt Alexandra call Atticus?

2. What does Jem mean when he says "It ain't right"?

3. What does Dill plan to do with his life?

4. Miss Maudie normally gives the children a small cake each. What does she do this time?

5. What special thing do the people do to show their appreciation to Atticus the next morning?

6. What does Mr. Ewell say and do to Atticus?

7. Does Miss Maudie think that it is an accident that Atticus was appointed by the judge to defend Tom Robinson?

8. What kind of person does Miss Maudie say that Atticus is?

9. Why does it say that Dill makes rabbit-bites?

10. What is Aunt Alexandra's response to the children's going to court?

Answers

1. Aunt Alexandra calls Atticus "Brother."

2. Jem means that it is not right that Tom was convicted.

3. Dill says that he plans to be a clown who laughs at people. He does not think he can change the way things are and, he prefers to laugh, not cry.

4. She gives Jem a slice from the big cake.

5. They bring him all kinds of food.

6. Mr. Ewell spits in Atticus's face and says he will get even.

7. Miss Maudie says that the judge purposely chose Atticus to defend Tom. Usually the judge would have selected a new, beginning lawyer for this type of case.

8. Miss Maudie says that Atticus is a person who does the unpleasant work for others.

9. It means that Dill eats with his front teeth.

10. Aunt Alexandra says that the children should not have been there wallowing in the trial.

Suggested Essay Topics

1. How did many people show their appreciation to Atticus? What does Atticus say and do when he sees their response to him?

2. What did Miss Maudie do for the children to make them feel better the morning after the trial? What did she say to them that made them feel better? Do you think she believed what she told them? Why do you believe this way?

Chapter 23

Summary

Atticus, Jem and Scout discuss the trial and Mr. Ewell. Atticus talks with them about the jury system in Maycomb. After Aunt Alexandra forbids Scout to play with Walter Cunningham, Jem shares his secret (a chest hair) with Scout. He also shares his philosophy of the kinds of folks there are in the world. They discuss Old Family and Scout reaches her conclusion: "there's just one kind of folks. Folks." Jem has also figured out that Boo stays inside because he wants to do so.

Analysis

Chapter 23 shows Scout and Jem trying to figure out the intricate construction of the community that they have been learning so much about lately.

The lesson Scout receives in this chapter proves to be extremely upsetting to her. Alexandra refuses to allow her to invite Walter Cunningham to their home. When Alexandra calls Walter "trash," Scout loses control and Jem leads her sobbing to her room. Scout resists the idea that people are expected to act differently due to their class as strongly as she resists learning behavior that she is expected to adopt because she's female. Jem explains that Aunty is "trying to make you a lady."

Once again the Ewells prove how dangerous ignorance can be. Their prejudice is sweeping, they "hate and despise the colored folk." And now they feel the same about Atticus for making them appear foolish. Bob Ewell responds by make crude and raving threats to Atticus, which Atticus receives with his usual grace and gentility.

In Chapter 23 Harper Lee continues to employ stylistic devices in her writing. *Foreshadowing* is used when Atticus says after the verdict, "this may be the shadow of a beginning." *Repetition* is used when Atticus asks Jem "to stand in Bob Ewell's shoes a minute"; when he tells Scout, "Not time to worry yet..."; and when Jem says again that "It ain't right." The chapter begins with *humor* when Atticus says, "I wish Bob Ewell wouldn't chew tobacco." Some examples of the 1930s Southern *dialect* occur in the speech of Mr. Bob Ewell. For example, Mr. Ewell asks, "Too proud to fight, you nigger-lovin' bastard?" All conflicts are not resolved by Chapter 23 in *To Kill a Mockingbird*, a novel with a *progressive plot*.

All of the drama and turmoil associated with the trial have given the children a new perspective on Boo Radley. Jem concludes the chapter by saying, "I think I'm beginning to understand why Boo Radley's stayed shut up...it's because he *wants* to stay inside."

Study Questions

1. What is Atticus's response when the children ask him to borrow a gun?

2. What is a *hung jury*?

3. The jury contained white males from outside Maycomb. What are some missing groups?

4. What humorous remark does Atticus make when Ewell spits in his face?

5. Scout believes that Aunt Alexandra wants to help her choose something. What is this?

6. Do you think Tom could get a fair trial with a jury of white males from outside Maycomb? Why?

7. What is Atticus' response when he was asked if he is afraid to fight?

8. Atticus says that one type of person is trash. Who was this?

9. Why could Miss Maudie not serve on a jury?

10. What does Aunt Alexandra call Walter Cunningham that angers Scout?

Answers

1. He responds "Nonsense."

2. A *hung jury* is one that cannot reach an agreement.

3. The Maycomb jury includes no woman, no "black man," and no Maycomb resident.

4. He says that he wished Bob Ewell did not chew tobacco

5. Aunt Alexandra seems to want to choose Scout's friends.

6. No, because they are not his peers.

7. Atticus says he is not afraid but too old to fight.

8. Trash is a white person who cheats a "black man."

9. Miss Maudie cannot serve because she is a woman.

10. Aunt Alexandra calls Walter trash.

Suggested Essay Topics

1. What were the four kinds of people in the world according to Jem? According to Jem's grouping system, where would Little Chuck Little who helped calm Miss Caroline when she saw the cootie be placed? Do you agree with Jem that the Finch family in Maycomb was in a different group than the Ewell family? Why?

2. Mr. Ewell spat in Atticus's face. What were some reasons Atticus did not fight back? Which man had greater courage?

Chapter 24

Summary

New Characters:

Mrs. Grace Merriweather, Mrs. Perkins, and Mrs. Farrow: *women in attendance at Aunt Alexandra's missionary circle meeting*

Chapter 24 describes the women's missionary circle meeting and the disruptions which occur. Aunt Alexandra has asked Calpurnia and Scout to help with serving at the event. Scout becomes the butt of two jokes. When Scout then asks Mrs. Merriweather about the topic of the meeting, the focus is drawn from Scout for a while. She begins to tell about J. Grimes Everett and his ministry to the Mrunas.

The topic of conversation moves to Tom Robinson and his family. Mrs. Merriweather says that she believes if the white folks can forgive that "darky's wife," things will blow over in Maycomb.

Mrs. Farrow says that she believes "no lady is safe in her bed these nights." Mrs. Farrow says that she has shared that information with Mr. Hutson and he agrees with her.

Mrs. Merriweather criticizes the good but misguided people who thought they were doing right "but all they did was stir 'em up." She begins to complain about Sophy, her maid. Mrs. Merriweather says that the only reason she keeps Sophy as an employee is because the depression is on and Sophy needs the $1.25 per week that she pays her. Miss Maudie remarks that Mr. Merriweather does not have trouble eating the food that Sophy cooks. Mrs. Merriweather claims not to understand.

Perfect hostess that she is, Aunt Alexandra begins to pass the food and change the subject, but Mrs. Merriweather begins an attack on Mrs. Roosevelt who tries "to sit with 'em."

Scout is thinking of Calpurnia and Calpurnia's words to Miss Rachel's cook. Calpurnia tells the cook that Tom is despondent and that Atticus has done all he can to help. Just then a door slams as Atticus returns home. He speaks to the ladies and asks Alexandra to come into the kitchen with him. Miss Maudie and Scout also go into the kitchen.

Atticus has come for Calpurnia. He has just found out that guards have shot Tom Robinson as he is trying to escape and Atticus wants Calpurnia to go with him to tell Tom's widow.

Miss Maudie orders Scout to stop shaking and tells Alexandra that they have left the women alone long enough. The three go back into the living room and the meeting goes on as if nothing happened.

Analysis

Miss Maudie proves her strength and intelligence once again when she confronts Mrs. Merriweather. Mrs. Merriweather has just said that Atticus is misguided and that the only reason she keeps Sophy is because Sophy "needs her dollar and a quarter every week she can get it." Miss Maudie remarks the Merriweathers do not have trouble eating Sophy's cooking, or Mr. Merriweather's "food doesn't

stick going down." She is not afraid to reveal Mrs. Merriweather's hypocracy.

In this chapter Scout learns that the ability to control one's emotions is necessary not only to become a young lady, but to achieve a level of maturity as a human being. She must struggle with this several times throughout the chapter. Miss Maudie tells Scout to "Stop that shaking." Alexandra, Miss Maudie, and Scout continue with what must be done without regard for themselves and their feelings. At the beginning of the meeting Scout describes how she "sat quietly, having conquered my hands by tightly gripping the arms of the chair…" and waited for someone to speak to her.

The ladies of the missionary circle prove how hypocritical and dangerous social rules can be. Mrs. Merriweather clearly puts her maid Sophy in a different category from her family. She is very opposed to "misguided people" who "stir 'em up." It is, of course, Atticus—a character-against-society—to whom she is referring. Although Scout is clearly not a part of this society, she recognizes that she "...must soon enter this world, where on its surface fragrant ladies rocked slowly, fanned gently, and drank cool water."

Through stylistic devices, Harper Lee creates a visual picture of the circle meeting with the talk that goes along with it. One device used by Lee is the *innuendo.* For example, Scout tells Miss Stephanie that she wants to grow up to be a lady; the implication is that Miss Stephanie is not. Lee uses *repetition* in her writing to drive home a point. Miss Maudie tells Aunt Alexandra that Atticus is being paid the highest form of respect; the people are trusting him to do right, a point brought out before in *To Kill a Mockingbird. Humor* is an important part of the chapter. One example is when Scout is asked where her pants are. She replies that they are under her dress. *Irony* is evident when the women in the missionary group behave in a cruel manner to Scout, their maids, and even one another. They are concerned with the Mrunas when there are groups in need in Maycomb. They overlook the "sin and squalor" (*alliteration*) at home and sought to get rid of the sin and squalor abroad. It is also ironic that Mrs. Merriweather says that the people should forgive Tom Robinson's wife.

Aunt Alexandra again demonstrates *sympathy.* Earlier the reader saw Aunt Alexandra show sympathy to Atticus after the verdict was given; this time her sympathy is in response to the death of Tom Robinson.

Study Questions

1. Where does the women's missionary circle hold its meeting?
2. Where are Dill and Jem?
3. During what month does the chapter take place?
4. Why is Scout not allowed to go with Dill and Jem?
5. What special group are the women studying?

6.   Who is conducting the study?

7.   Mrs. Merriweather tries to make Scout look bad in front of the others. She says Scout might want to be a lawyer since she has "already commenced going to court." What does Scout say she wants to be when she grows up?

8.   What bad news does Atticus bring home?

9.   Mrs. Merriweather keeps saying there is someone the ladies needed to forgive. Who is it?

10. Who does Atticus take with him to Mrs. Robinson's?

Answers

1.   The women's missionary group meets in the Finch home.

2.   Dill and Jem are swimming at Barker's Eddy.

3.   The chapter takes place in late August.

4.   Scout cannot go with the boys since they are swimming naked.

5.   The women are studying the Mrunas.

6.   Mrs. Merriweather is conducting the study.

7.   Scout says she wants to grow up to be a lady.

8.   The bad news is that Tom had attempted escape and had been killed by guards.

9.   She thought the women should forgive Mrs. Robinson.

10. Atticus takes Calpurnia with him.

Suggested Essay Topics

1.   Aunt Alexandra is trying to teach Scout to be a lady. From what went on at the meeting, what is a lady, according to Miss Maudie's example? according to Aunt Alexandra's example? according to Scout's thoughts?

2.   What is a missionary circle? Describe the women's missionary meeting. Is there any irony evident at the meeting? Explain.

Chapter 25

New Characters:

Helen Robinson: *Tom's wife*

Sam and a little girl: *Tom and Helen's children*

Summary

When Chapter 25 opens, Scout and Jem are on the back porch. Scout is playing with a roly-poly. Jem orders her not to kill the creature. Scout remembers what Jem had told her about his trip to Mrs. Helen Robinson's home.

On the way to the Robinson Place, Calpurnia and Atticus pick up Dill and Jem. Since much happens outside while they are still in the car, they are able to tell Scout exactly what happens. Sam goes to get his mother, Helen. When she asks them in, she sees their faces, knows what has happened, and faints. Atticus and Calpurnia stay inside a long time.

Mr. Underwood writes a bitter editorial in the *Maycomb Tribune*, comparing Tom's death to the "senseless slaughter of songbirds."

The chapter concludes with Ewell's remarks about the death of Tom Robinson: "it made one down and about two more to go."

Analysis

Chapter 25 proves that Maycomb's difficult time did not end with the trial. Tom's death almost seems to prove that it is impossible to oppose or to change the unwritten laws of society—no matter how unjust or dangerous they may be. Mr. Underwood shows great bravery and emphasizes this theme when he does not hesitate to write angrily in his paper about the injustices that have been brought upon the Robinson family—particularly Tom—by the community.

Atticus shows a different kind of bravery when he goes to inform Helen Robinson of her husband's death. This job is one of the most difficult one could have to do. Once again, Atticus shows bravery also in ignoring Bob Ewell's threats. Bob Ewell, on the other hand, proves his ignorance and insensitivity by responding to the news of Tom's death with the phrase "…one down and about two more to go."

The *theme of the mockingbird* is very evident in this chapter. There is a hint of that theme at the beginning of the chapter when Jem will not allow Scout to kill the roly-poly. The theme is very explicit when Mr. Underwood writes of the sin of killing a songbird in his editorial.

The *theme of maturation* continues to be important in *To Kill a Mockingbird*. The reader is made aware that Jem is cognizant of the meaning of many of the events of the past few weeks. They have aged him. Scout remarks on the change: "It was probably just a stage he was going through, and I wished he would hurry up and get through it." At another point Scout remarks upon Jem's charity: "Jem was the one who was getting more like a girl every day, not I."

Study Questions

1. What does Jem order Scout not to kill?

2. Why do Jem and Dill go with Atticus to the Robinson Place?

3. What condition does Atticus make for the two boys to go?

4. What game are the children playing at the Robinson Place?

5. What tender gesture does Atticus make while waiting for Helen?

6. What is Helen's reaction to seeing Atticus's face?

7. What does Mr. Underwood do to confront society?

8. To what does Mr. Underwood compare Tom Robinson?

9. What does Mr. Ewell say when he hears of Tom's death?

10. Why does Scout not tell Atticus what Mr. Ewell said?

Answers

1. Jem orders Scout not to kill a roly-poly bug.

2. Dill and Jem are on their way back from swimming when they meet Atticus and flag him down to get a ride. He picks them up, but tells them that he is not going straight home.

3. He tells the boys that they must stay in the car.

4. The children at the Robinson Place are playing marbles.

5. Atticus helps one of Tom's little girls down the steps.

6. Helen Robinson faints after seeing Atticus's face.

7. Mr. Underwood writes an editorial to confront society.

8. Mr. Underwood compares Tom to a songbird.

9. Mr. Ewell says, "One down and two to go" when he hears of Tom's death.

10. Jem says he would never speak to Scout again if she told. He says Mr. Ewell was hot air.

Suggested Essay Topics

1. Tell about Mr. Underwood's editorial. To what does he compare Tom? Is this a good analogy? Why?

2. Compare and contrast the Robinson Place with the Radley Place. Do ghosts exist at both places? Explain.

Chapter 26

New Character:

Miss Gates: *Scout's third-grade teacher*

Summary

Scout is in third grade and Jem is in seventh when this chapter begins. Scout is walking home from school by herself now. She finds that the Radley Place does not hold the terror that it did for her, but she still watches for Mr. Arthur when she passes.

Mrs. Gates uses current events in her third-grade class. On this day the teacher discusses the Jews, Hitler, and the harm that he has done. Scout begins to draw parallels between the Jews and the oppressed in Maycomb. Scout remembers that Miss Gates was talking after the trial about teaching "em a lesson, and how they were getting way above themselves, and the next thing they will think they can marry us." When she asks Jem about it, he says he never wants to hear about that courthouse again. Atticus tells her that Jem thinks he is trying to forget something, but he is actually storing it to think about later.

Analysis

In Chapter 26, Scout is once again pitted against her teacher as she recognizes her hypocrisy. With a childish clarity of vision, Scout recognizes injustice, but she is confused by the way people cover this up. She goes to Jem to try to understand it all, but he becomes angry and will not discuss it with her. Atticus explains that Jem is trying to forget, but he is actually storing it in his mind until he can sort it out.

It is ironic that Miss Gates opposes what Hitler is doing to the Jews, but she herself is opposed to Tom Robinson's being acquitted. Scout tells Jem that she overheard Miss Gates saying after the trial that "it's time somebody taught 'em a lesson, they were gettin' way above themselves, an' the next thing they think they can do is marry us."

The *motif* of education is continued in Chapter 26. Scout returns to school; she is now in third grade. Jem is in seventh grade and Scout often discusses things with him since she values his advice. Scout's true education, however, continues to be outside the classroom. It is a sign of Scout's own maturity that she is beginning to teach herself. When her teacher confuses her, and Jem refuses to help her, she tries to sort things out on her own. Another sign that she is growing is that she is no longer plagued with childish fears of the Radley Place.

Harper Lee makes use of *symbolism*. The tree is swelling around the cement patch and seeking to dislodge it. Mr. Radley put the patch on the healthy tree, just as his father tried to change his healthy son Arthur. Perhaps Arthur will reject the alteration just as the tree is rejecting its alteration.

Lee employs the *simile* when she compares the events of the summer hanging over them to "smoke in a closed room."

Study Questions

1. What grade is Jem in in this chapter?

2. What grade is Scout in in this chapter?

3. How does Scout feel about the Radley Place now?

4. What newspaper does Miss Gates dislike?

5. What term does Miss Gates say means equal rights for everyone?

6. When does Scout see Atticus scowl?

7. Why is Jem trying to gain weight? How?

8. How does Scout define democracy?

9. What had Scout heard Miss Gates say on the courthouse steps?

10. Why does Atticus say that Jem would not talk about the courthouse?

Answers

1. Jem is in the seventh grade in this chapter.

2. Scout is in the third grade in this chapter.

3. Scout still thinks the Radley Place is gloomy, but she is not terrified of it.

4. Miss Gates dislikes The Grit Paper.

5. Miss Gates says democracy means equal rights for everyone.

6. Scout sees Atticus scowl when Hitler is mentioned on the radio.

7. Jem is trying to gain weight by eating bananas and milk. He needs to gain 25 pounds in two years to play football.

8. Democracy is defined as "Equal rights for all, special privileges for none."

9. Scout had heard Miss Gates say derogatory things about black people on the courthouse steps. She said things about teaching "'em a lesson, and how they were getting way above themselves, and the next thing they will think they can marry us."

10. Atticus says that Jem is trying to forget, but that actually he is storing the information until he can sort things out.

Suggested Essay Topics

1. Why did Miss Gates use current events in her class? Know-

ing what Miss Gates said on the courthouse steps, are there any inconsistencies in what she says in the classroom and what she does and says outside the class? How is this similar or different from Atticus?

2.   Compare a democracy and a dictatorship. How are they different?

Chapter 27

Summary

New Characters:

Ruth Jones: *the welfare woman who says Mr. Ewell accused Atticus of getting his job*

Mrs. Crenshaw: *the local seamstress*

The Barber sisters: *two deaf and elderly women who live together*

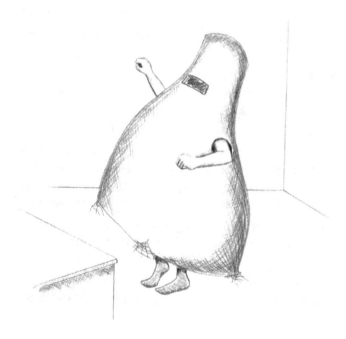

Chapter 27 describes three unusual events: Mr. Ewell gets a job and accuses Atticus of causing him to lose it; someone tries to break into Judge Taylor's house; and when Helen Robinson goes to work for Link Deas, the Ewell family throws rocks at her as she walks past their home. Mr. Deas faces Mr. Ewell down and tells him to leave Helen alone.

Two changes have come to Maycomb. The first change is that the National Recovery Act Signs are being removed from the stores. The second change is that Halloween will be an organized affair because of the pranks played on the Barber sisters last year. Scout will be a ham in this year's pageant and will be escorted to the event by her brother.

Analysis

In Chapter 27, Bob Ewell makes a futile attempt to become part of the Maycomb community. This is viewed as unnatural and has turbulent results. He loses the job and blames Atticus, although Atticus has nothing to do with it. Ewell also continues to punish those he feels are responsible for his humiliation by breaking into Judge Taylor's house.

Ewell's cowardly attempts to revenge are extended even to Robinson's widow. She has been given a job which leads her past the Ewell house and he taunts her and follows her. Although her position in society does not give her the strength to defend herself, her employer, Link Deas, shows bravery in defending her. He threatens to bring in the law—the bastion society—and to stop Ewell's petty vigilante revenge attempts once and for all.

Atticus is still trying to understand things from Robert Ewell's perspective. Atticus "crawls in Ewell's skin" and explains to Aunt Alexandra why Ewell is not satisfied with the court decision.

Foreshadowing is used to create *suspense* as Scout says, "Thus began our longest journey together" and when Aunt Alexandra says, "somebody just walked over my grave."

Study Questions

1. What does Mrs. Jones say Mr. Ewell said when he lost his job?

2. When does Judge Taylor hear a strange noise?

3. Why does Helen walk a mile out of her way to get to work?

4. Who defends Helen against Mr. Ewell?

5. What noise did Judge Taylor hear?

6. During what month does this chapter take place?

7. What is Scout's costume for the pageant?

8. What are the nicknames for the Barber sisters?

9. What trick is played on the Barber sisters?

10. Who escorts Scout to the pageant?

Answers

1. Mr. Ewell says that Atticus got his job.

2. Judge Taylor hears a strange sound on Sunday night.

3. Helen walks a mile out of her way to avoid the Ewell Place.

4. Mr. Link Deas tells Mr. Ewell to leave Helen alone.

5. Someone cut Judge Taylor's screen causing the noise.

6. This chapter takes place in October.

7. Scout is a ham for the pageant.

8. The children call the Barbers Tutti and Frutti.

9. The furniture from downstairs was put in the cellar while they slept.

10. Jem escorts Scout to the pageant.

Suggested Essay Topics

1. Why was Robert Ewell bitter, according to Atticus? How did he show his bitterness?

2. Compare and contrast the break-in on the Barber sisters' house and the attempted break-in on Judge Taylor's house.

3. Describe in detail Scout's costume for the pageant.

Chapter 28

Summary

New Character:

Dr. Reynolds: *the family physician who examines Jem and Scout after the pageant*

Chapter 28 describes events before, during, and after the pageant. Jem and Scout are frightened by Cecil Jacobs on the way to the Halloween celebration. Scout makes a late entrance on stage during the pageant. The children are attacked by Bob Ewell on the way home, but someone comes to their aid and carries Jem home. Scout follows. Aunt Alexandra calls the doctor who finds that Jem's arm is broken. Sheriff Tate finds Mr. Ewell lying under the oak with a knife in his chest.

Analysis

Chapter 28 shows Ewell sinking to a new low in his desperate attempts for revenge. Because he lives outside of society he cannot

utilize the law. Because of his ignorance, he cannot engage Atticus in rational discussion. Instead, he strikes out at those who Atticus cares about the most—his innocent and vulnerable children.

Harper Lee uses *a false climax* in her writing. On the way to the pageant, the children are frightened by someone. The reader expects danger but it turns out to be only Cecil Jacobs, a boy in Scout's class.

The *theme* of ghosts and the supernatural is evident from the beginning of the chapter. The first lines refer to the Radley Place and Halloween—with no moon. Harper Lee—through Scout—describes the scary walk to the high school auditorium and the even more frightening walk home.

The *theme of bravery* is evident in this chapter. The children show bravery through the walk to and from the auditorium, but the real hero—who is not revealed explicitly at this time—is the one who assists them in the scuffle after the pageant.

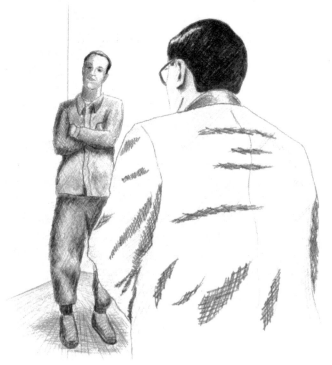

Study Questions

1. What is the weather like on Halloween night?
2. Who frightens the children on the way to the auditorium?
3. What is Cecil Jacob's costume for the pageant?
4. How much money does Scout have and how many things can she do with it?
5. Why does Scout miss her cue in the pageant?
6. Why are the children among the last ones to leave the auditorium?
7. Why does Scout wear her costume home?
8. Why can Jem see Scout in the dark?
9. How many people scuffle under the tree?
10. Who does Sheriff Tate find has been killed in the scuffle?

Answers

1. The weather is warm and the sky cloudy and dark.
2. Cecil Jacobs frightens the children on the way to the pageant.
3. Cecil Jacobs is a cow in the pageant.
4. Scout has 30¢ so she can do six things at the Halloween celebration.
5. Scout misses her cue because she is asleep.
6. Scout does not want to leave until most people are gone because she is embarrassed by her performance and does not want to talk about it.
7. Scout wants to wear her costume because she can hide her mortification under it.
8. Jem can see Scout because the fat streaks in the costume are painted with shiny paint.
9. Four people scuffle under the tree.
10. The sheriff finds Mr. Ewell has been killed in the struggle.

Suggested Essay Topics

1. Describe the Maycomb Halloween celebration.

2. What events contributed most to the confrontation that occurs after the celebration?

Chapter 29

Summary

After Aunt Alexandra goes to bed, the sheriff, the doctor, Atticus, and Scout discuss the night's events. Only after Scout tells the story, does she notice Boo in the corner. She speaks to him face to face for the first time.

Analysis

Boo Radley has made the choice to appear in public to save the lives of the Finch children. His fight to remain apart from society has been subjected to his fight for right. Ironically, this is the opposite decision from the one Atticus had to make in defending Tom Robinson. Atticus' decision to fight for right didn't draw him into society but rather threatened to cut him off from it. For Boo, entering society is a powerful act of bravery.

Stylistic devices continue to be evident in Lee's writing. Aunt Alexandra makes mention again of the *foreshadowing* she had of the attack. "I had a feeling about this tonight—I—this is my fault…" Mr. Tate's response is a *simile*: "why, if we followed our feelings all the time we'd be like cats chasin' their tails." Scout's description of Boo is a *hyperbole* (exaggeration): "hands that had never seen the sun.…" Harper Lee uses *imagery* in her writing when she describes Boo Radley. At last the reader has an accurate mental image of this recluse, with his white face, his hollow cheeks, and his colorless, gray eyes.

Study Questions

1. What is Atticus's one sign of inner turmoil?

2. Why does Mr. Tate say it is all right that Alexandra had not heeded her feeling?

3. Why does Atticus want Scout to raise her head when she talks?

4. Why don't the children go back for Scout's shoes?

5. What does Scout call out to Cecil Jacobs?

6. Why do Atticus and Alexandra not hear the sounds outside?

7. Why does Mr. Tate say Mr. Ewell acted the way that he did?

8. How does Scout know that she is under the tree?

9. Who brings Jem into the house?

10. What does Scout say to the man who rescued Jem and her?

Answers

1. The strong line of his jaw melts a little.

2. He says if we heeded all our feelings, we would be like cats chasing our tails.

3. He wants Scout to raise her head so Mr. Tate can hear.

4. The children don't go back because they see the lights go off.

5. She calls out that Cecil is a big, fat hen.

6. They were listening to their radios.

7. Mr. Tate says that Mr. Ewell acted the way he did because he was mean.

8. Scout knows she is under the tree because the sand feels cool.

9. Boo Radley brings Jem to the house.

10. Scout says, "Hey, Boo."

Suggested Essay Topics

1. Describe what happened after the children arrive home. Why did Boo decide to stay at the Finch home instead of sneaking back home? What feelings do you think Boo was experiencing?

2. Describe Boo Radley. Compare and contrast his true description with the description that the children held of him in Part One.

3. In Part One Scout called Arthur Radley, "Boo." Miss Maudie tells her to call him, "Arthur." She thinks of him as Mr. Arthur on her way home from third grade. When she sees him for the first time, she calls him, "Boo." What is the significance of each of these names?

Chapter 30

Summary

Chapter 30 takes place in Jem's bedroom until Dr. Reynolds appears with a package. Then Boo, Scout, Atticus, and Sheriff Tate go to the porch. Atticus and Sheriff Tate argue about Ewell's death. Atticus says that Jem killed Ewell, but Tate says that Ewell fell on his knife. At last they all agree to Tate's story. They decide on this story to protect Boo and to let the dead bury the dead.

Analysis

The *theme* of the mockingbird is prominent in Chapter 30. Scout makes an *analogy*, or a comparison, between putting Boo on trial and killing a mockingbird; she says: "it'd be sort of like shootin' a mockingbird, wouldn't it?"

In Chapter 30 we see that perhaps the best way to decide the fate of someone who has always separated himself from society is without the regular societal procedures. It would be possible for Atticus and Heck Tate to have another trial to determine the cause of Bob Ewell's death. Calling in the law would certainly be the conventional legal method. They choose to rely on a different form of justice, however.

Mr. Tate and Atticus know that Boo does not stand a chance against the community. One man is already dead because of Ewell. By his "investigation" of Ewell's death, Mr. Tate tries to make amends for his earlier mistakes which cost Tom his life. Atticus protects Boo by not making him appear in court. The reader sees

Atticus willing to allow his son to face the charges of murder in order to hold his head up and to have no whispers about him. All these actions are brave ones.

Repetition figures prominently in the chapter. Atticus wants, in effect, for others to know that Jem lives in the dark as he does in the light—a statement reminiscent of Miss Maudie's earlier comments about Atticus.

Study Questions

1. What is in the doctor's package?
2. Why do they take Boo on the front porch?
3. In what order do they go out on the front porch?
4. What does the sheriff say had happened to Mr. Ewell?
5. What does Atticus say had happened to Mr. Ewell?
6. What comparison does Scout make with Boo?
7. For what does Atticus thank Boo?
8. How does Scout try to cheer Atticus up after Mr. Tate leaves?
9. What kind of knife was used to kill Mr. Ewell?
10. Where does the sheriff say he had gotten the switchblade?

Answers

1. The doctor carries medical supplies.
2. They take Boo to the front porch because they think he will be more comfortable in the dark.
3. Mr. Tate, then Atticus, then Scout and Boo together.
4. The sheriff says Mr. Ewell had fallen on his knife.
5. Atticus thinks Jem killed him in self-defense.
6. Scout compares Boo to a mockingbird.
7. Atticus thanks Boo for his children.
8. Scout tries to cheer Atticus with hugs and kisses.
9. A kitchen knife was used to kill Mr. Ewell.

10. The sheriff says he had gotten the switchblade from a drunk.

Suggested Essay Topics

1. Tell Atticus's story of the murder and what he thought should be done.

2. What did Sheriff Tate want to do about the murder and why?

Chapter 31

Summary

Chapter 31 tells of Boo's visiting Jem and of Scout's taking him home. She remembers the past and realizes that they have in effect been Boo's children through time. She goes to Jem's room and falls asleep as Atticus reads to her. She knows, as Atticus tucks her in, that he will be there through the night and in the morning.

Analysis

The *denouement* (ending) of *To Kill a Mockingbird* is a closed, settled one. There is nothing else to be resolved. All the *conflicts* are ended: Boo is a friend, Ewell is dead, Scout has given in to sleep, and for the moment the family is safe from society and its pressures.

The *maturational motif* is evident again when Scout says that "there wasn't much else left for us to learn, except possibly algebra." Scout has matured and has learned to stand in others shoes. The *repetition* of a statement by Atticus is important here: "you never really know a man until you stand in his shoes." This statement serves to weave Part One and Part Two together.

Study Questions

1. Why does Boo go inside the Finch house again?

2. What book is Atticus reading?

3. Why does Scout walk with Arthur to his home?

4. Why does she ask Boo to take her arm?

5. Why does Scout go to sleep before the story is over?

6. Why does the doctor put a tent over Jem?

7. Why is Atticus reading the book?

8. What does Atticus say most people are like when you finally see them?

9. What makes you think Atticus does not believe Scout when she says she is not afraid?

10. What makes Scout sad in thinking back on all the gifts Boo had given them?

Answers

1. Boo Radley goes inside the Finch house again to see Jem.

2. Atticus reads *The Gray Ghost.*

3. Scout walks with Arthur to his home because he asked her to do so.

4. She asks Boo to take her arm so if Miss Stephanie looks from her window, she will see a gentleman escorting a lady.

5. The room is warm, the rain is soft, Atticus's knee is snug, and the voice is deep so Scout goes to sleep.

6. The tent is to protect Jem's arm from the cover.

7. Atticus reads the book because he has never read it.

8. Atticus says most people are nice when you finally see them.

9. When Atticus raises his eyebrows, the reader knows he does not believe Scout.

10. Scout is sad because she remembers that they had given Boo nothing.

Suggested Essay Topics

1. What could be seen from Arthur's porch?

2. Are there indications in the chapter that Boo is sick and will die?

Sample Analytical Paper Topics

The following paper topics are designed to test your understanding of the novel as a whole and to analyze important themes and literary devices. Following each question is a sample outline to help get you started.

Topic #1

The theme of the mockingbird is an important one in *To Kill a Mockingbird*. Write a paper on the mockingbird theme in Harper Lee's only book. Be sure to tell what a mockingbird is and tell exactly why both Boo and Tom are mockingbirds. Are fears and superstitions associated with the mockingbird theme, with Boo, and/or with Tom? Explain your answer.

Outline

I. Thesis Statement: *Harper Lee uses the mockingbird theme with both Boo and Tom as examples and with fears and superstitions attached to the mockingbird and both characters.*

II. Definition of a mockingbird

    A. Songbird

    B. Gives its music

    C. Expects nothing in return

    D. Does no harm

    E. Sin to kill mockingbird

III. Boo

    A. Like the songbird

    B. Gives gifts in tree and in end protects children

    C. Expects no gifts or favors in return

    D. Does no harm

    E. Sin to harm or kill Boo

IV. Tom

    A. Like the songbird

    B. Gives gifts of labor

    C. Expects no gifts or favors in return

    D. Does no harm

    E. Sin to harm or kill Tom

V. Superstitions attached to each

    A. Mockingbird

        1. Sin to kill

        2. Spends life giving

    B. Boo

        1. Rumors spread about him

        2. Fear attached to him and the Radley Place

    C. Tom

        1. Rumors spread about him

        2. Fears associated with him and his race

            a. "No lady safe in her bed" (Mrs. Farrow)

            b. "Sin to kill a cripple" (Underwood)

Topic #2

Both Atticus and Bob Ewell are important characters in the novel. Compare and contrast these important characters.

Outline

I. Thesis Statement: *In the novel* To Kill a Mockingbird *there are similarities and differences between Atticus and Bob Ewell, but the differences outweigh the similarities.*

II. Similarities

    A. Fathers

    B. Single parents

    C. Set examples for their children

III. Differences

    A. Atticus Finch

        1. Same in public as private

        2. Set example of honesty and concern for others to children

        3. Did not use corporal punishment

        4. Works as lawyer

    B. Bob Ewell

        1. Does evil works in secrecy

            a. Scares Helen Robinson when she is alone

            b. Cuts judge's screen

            c. Attacks children at night when they are alone

        2. Sets contentious example for children

        3. Beats children

        4. Does not hold job

Topic #3

Atticus teaches many lessons to his children. What are some of the lessons that Atticus taught? How does he teach his lessons? Cite examples from the novel.

Outline

I. Thesis Statement: *Atticus teaches many lessons to his children through his examples and through his patient lessons.*

II. Lessons

    A. Answer children when they ask you something

    B. Do not hurt the defenseless

    C. Be the same in public as in private

    D. Use compromise when possible

    E. Try to crawl into someone else's skin

III. Means of instruction

    A. Tells brother to do so and does himself

    B. Example

    C. Example

    D. Shows Scout how to do so by doing with her

    E. Mentions many, many times to children

Topic #4

Lee chooses Scout as narrator for the novel. In what way does it accomplish Lee's purpose to have a young, innocent narrator? Can she make a profound statement about the hypocrisy of society? Explain your answer.

Outline

I. Thesis Statement: *Through Scout's innocent point-of-view, the reader sees Maycomb society with its barriers of class, race, and sex.*

II. "Different kinds of folks"

    A. Jem

        1. Ordinary folks like the Finches and neighbors

        2. The Ewells

        3. The Cunninghams

        4. The Negroes

    B. Aunt Alexandra

        1. Heredity

        2. Shortcomings in other tribal groups

    C. Scout

        1. Says that "Folks is folks"

        2. Less prejudiced than most other characters

III. Sees evidence of racial differentiation

    A. Said Calpurnia was "supposed to use back door"

    B. Jury was white men from outside town

    C. Is told by Reverend Sykes that he "ain't ever seen any jury decide in favor of a colored man over a white man...."

IV. Sex lines in Maycomb

    A. Women not on a jury

    B. Expect girls to act and dress in a certain way

    C. Southern womanhood

SECTION FOUR

Bibliography

Etheridge, James and Kopola, Barbara, eds. *Contemporary Authors.*
   Detroit: Gale Research Company, 1966.

Lee, Harper. *To Kill A Mockingbird.* New York: Warner Books, 1960.

Nash, Jay Roberts and Ross, Stanley, eds. *The Motion Picture Guide,*
   Vol. 8. Chicago: Cinebooks, Inc. 1987.

MAXnotes® are simply the best – but don't just take our word for it...

"... I have told every bookstore in the area to carry your MAXnotes. They are the only notes I recommend to my students. There is no comparison between MAXnotes and all other notes ..."
— *High School Teacher & Reading Specialist, Arlington High School, Arlington, MA*

"... I discovered the MAXnotes when a friend loaned me her copy of the *MAXnotes for Romeo and Juliet*. The book really helped me understand the story. Please send me a list of stores in my area that carry the MAXnotes. I would like to use more of them ..."
— *Student, San Marino, CA*

"... The two MAXnotes titles that I have used have been very, very useful in helping me understand the subject matter reviewed. Thank you for creating the MAXnotes series ..."
— *Student, Morrisville, PA*

"... I got 50% more out of the book that simply would have been lost. Way to go, MAXnotes!"
— *Student, Campbell, CA*

"... These notes really helped me study! I don't know what I would have done without them!"
— *Student, Philadelphia, PA*